THE

WORLD

FOR IAN. SOON. — TAN x

AUTHOR NOTE

Our world is vast, strong, fragile and wildly beautiful, and compressing its richness into a billion books would be impossible. *I ♥ the World* is a mere slip of the complexities and diversity to be found from the tip of Mount Everest to the depths of the Mariana Trench. The purpose of this book is to spark curiosity and adventure, and to hopefully encourage environmental awareness (and a love of noodles). The inclusions and inspiration contained within are designed to incite harmony and understanding and to forge the traveler in us all.
- Tania McCartney

THANK YOU

Huge thanks to publisher Melissa Kayser for her vision and to the team at HGT for their support, especially Megan Cuthbert, Nikki Lusk and Jessica Smith. To my extraordinary project editor Alice Barker for her insight and humour. And to my family and friends for their endless support and patience. Thanks, too, to all the adults who truly understand the value of travel for children.

I ♥ THE WORLD

A CELEBRATION OF LAND, SEA, FLORA, FAUNA AND PEOPLE AROUND THE GLOBE

TANIA MCCARTNEY

Hardie Grant
TRAVEL

CONTENTS

OUR WORLD

NORTH AMERICA

EUROPE

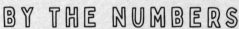

BY THE NUMBERS

SURFACE AREA: 197 million mi²/510 million km²
LAND AREA: 57 million mi²/149 million km²
COUNTRIES: 195
POPULATION: 7.7 billion people (2019)
BIGGEST CITY BY POPULATION: Tokyo, Japan
BIGGEST CITY BY AREA: New York City, USA
CONTINENTS: Seven
CIRCUMFERENCE: 24,901mi/40,075km
MADE UP OF: Mostly iron, oxygen and silicon
PLANET AGE: Around 4.54 billion years old!
TIME TO ORBIT THE SUN: 365.256 days
ATMOSPHERE: 78% nitrogen, 21% oxygen, 1% other
LAYERS: Crust, upper mantle, lower mantle, inner core and outer core
NATURAL SATELLITES: One very nice moon
GALAXY: The Milky Way

SOUTH AMERICA

ANTARCTICA

THE ARCTIC
CIRCLE
PAGE 30

ASIA
PAGE 62

AFRICA
PAGE 54

OCEANIA
PAGE 70

IT'S A BIG, BEAUTIFUL WORLD!

The world is a massive place and there's so much to explore! From the North Pole to tropical islands, you'll discover seven continents, five oceans and countless wonders in I ♥ the World.

Marvel at the people, cultures, foods and traditions. Learn all about the varieties of plants, animals and landscapes. Where is the longest mountain range on Earth? What about the largest desert? Do plants grow in Antarctica? The answers may surprise you!

Our land, sea and sky are brimming with color and life ... there's so much to love. Pack your sense of adventure as you explore and celebrate the variety, diversity and beauty of our incredible world.

OUR LAND

There are seven continents, with many landscapes – from deserts to tundra, rainforests to swamps, beaches to canyons, plateaus to mountains and Antarctic ice sheets over 1.2 miles (2 kilometers) thick! You can find all kinds of life, too – from the teensiest mouse to the largest tree. Be on the lookout for man-made structures, both ancient and new.

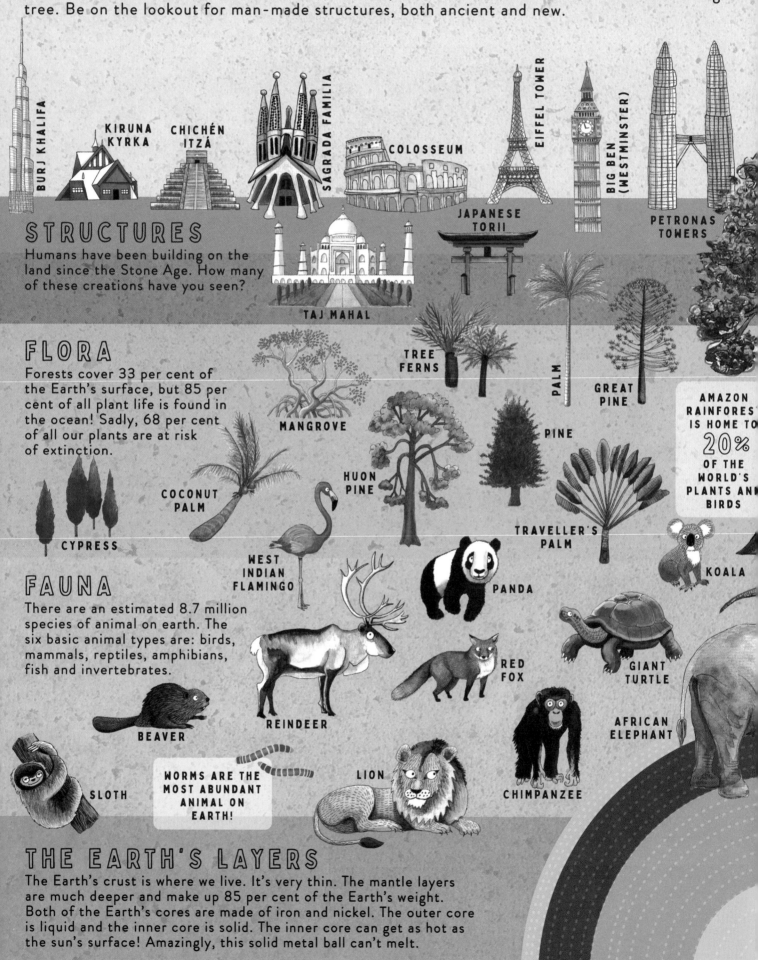

STRUCTURES

Humans have been building on the land since the Stone Age. How many of these creations have you seen?

BURJ KHALIFA

KIRUNA KYRKA

CHICHÉN ITZÁ

SAGRADA FAMILIA

COLOSSEUM

EIFFEL TOWER

BIG BEN (WESTMINSTER)

PETRONAS TOWERS

JAPANESE TORII

TAJ MAHAL

FLORA

Forests cover 33 per cent of the Earth's surface, but 85 per cent of all plant life is found in the ocean! Sadly, 68 per cent of all our plants are at risk of extinction.

MANGROVE

TREE FERNS

PALM

GREAT PINE

PINE

COCONUT PALM

HUON PINE

TRAVELLER'S PALM

KOALA

CYPRESS

WEST INDIAN FLAMINGO

PANDA

AMAZON RAINFOREST IS HOME TO 20% OF THE WORLD'S PLANTS AND BIRDS

FAUNA

There are an estimated 8.7 million species of animal on earth. The six basic animal types are: birds, mammals, reptiles, amphibians, fish and invertebrates.

BEAVER

REINDEER

RED FOX

GIANT TURTLE

AFRICAN ELEPHANT

SLOTH

WORMS ARE THE MOST ABUNDANT ANIMAL ON EARTH!

LION

CHIMPANZEE

THE EARTH'S LAYERS

The Earth's crust is where we live. It's very thin. The mantle layers are much deeper and make up 85 per cent of the Earth's weight. Both of the Earth's cores are made of iron and nickel. The outer core is liquid and the inner core is solid. The inner core can get as hot as the sun's surface! Amazingly, this solid metal ball can't melt.

LANDSCAPES

LARGEST CONTINENT: Asia (17 million mi²/44.5 million km²)
DRIEST INHABITED CONTINENT: Australia (Oceania)
WETTEST CONTINENT: South America
TALLEST POINT: Mount Everest (29,029ft/8848m)
LOWEST POINT: Dead Sea shoreline (1355ft/413m below sea level)
BIGGEST DESERT: The Antarctic desert (5.4 million mi²/14 million km²)
BIGGEST RAINFOREST: Amazon Rainforest (2.1 million mi²/5.5 million km²)
LARGEST ROCK: Mount Augustus (Burringurrah), Australia (35.5mi²/92km²)

GOLDEN GATE BRIDGE

SYDNEY OPERA HOUSE

TABRIZ BLUE MOSQUE

STONEHENGE

ST BASIL'S CATHEDRAL

FORBIDDEN CITY

HAGIA SOPHIA

ACROPOLIS

POPLAR

PANDANUS

EUCALYPTUS

SISAL

ACACIA

OAK

SMALL PINE

CACTUS

80% OF THE WORLD'S FORESTS HAVE BEEN CLEARED OR DAMAGED

BAOBAB

DRAGON BLOOD

MALLEE

GRASS TREE

GOANNA

AMERICAN BISON

EMPEROR PENGUIN

CAMEL

BILBY

BENGAL TIGER

ICELANDIC SHEEP

EURASIAN BROWN BEAR

RACCOON

CHITAL DEER

SPANISH FIGHTING BULL

KIWI

CRUST

UPPER MANTLE

LOWER MANTLE

OUTER CORE

INNER CORE

OUR OCEANS

PACIFIC OCEAN
63.8 MILLION MI²
(165.2 MILLION KM²)

ATLANTIC OCEAN
40.9 MILLION MI²
(106 MILLION KM²)

INDIAN OCEAN
26.5 MILLION MI²
(68.5 MILLION KM²)

SOUTHERN OCEAN
7.83 MILLION MI²
20.3 MILLION KM²

ARCTIC OCEAN
5.4 MILLION MI²
(14 MILLION KM²)

OCEAN OR SEA?

There are five oceans, and they make up 99 per cent of the Earth's living space. Their waters blur into seas, straits, gulfs, bays, fjords, bights, sounds, inlets and rivers. Around 70 per cent of the Earth is covered in water, and we've explored just five per cent of our oceans. Thanks to climate change, the Earth's sea levels continue to rise. If all the world's ice melted, they would rise 216 feet (66 meters), and we would lose countless coastal towns and cities.

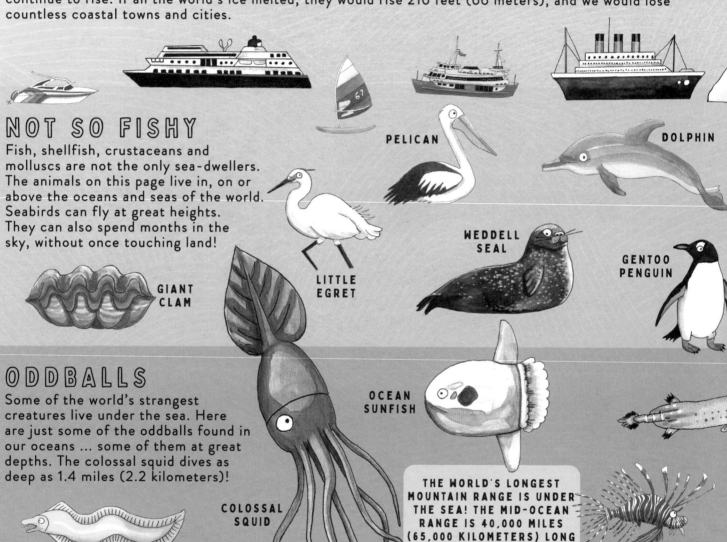

NOT SO FISHY

Fish, shellfish, crustaceans and molluscs are not the only sea-dwellers. The animals on this page live in, on or above the oceans and seas of the world. Seabirds can fly at great heights. They can also spend months in the sky, without once touching land!

PELICAN

DOLPHIN

LITTLE EGRET

GIANT CLAM

WEDDELL SEAL

GENTOO PENGUIN

ODDBALLS

Some of the world's strangest creatures live under the sea. Here are just some of the oddballs found in our oceans ... some of them at great depths. The colossal squid dives as deep as 1.4 miles (2.2 kilometers)!

OCEAN SUNFISH

COLOSSAL SQUID

MORAY EEL

THE WORLD'S LONGEST MOUNTAIN RANGE IS UNDER THE SEA! THE MID-OCEAN RANGE IS 40,000 MILES (65,000 KILOMETERS) LONG AND SNAKES THROUGH THREE OCEANS

LIONFISH

WHALES

Whales are found all over the globe, in all oceans and temperatures. There are two types of whale – toothed and baleen (no teeth). The blue whale is the largest baleen and the sperm whale is the largest toothed. Here are the world's largest whales, in order of size.

BLUE
98.5FT/30M

FIN
90FT/27.5M

ONLY 2.5% OF THE EARTH'S WATER IS FRESH

SOUTHERN ROYAL ALBATROSS

WATER, WATER EVERYWHERE

OCEAN SURFACE AREA: 139 million mi²/360 million km²
LARGEST OCEAN: Pacific Ocean (one third of Earth's surface)
LARGEST SEA: Philippine Sea (2.2 million mi²/5.7 million km²)
DEEPEST SPOT: Mariana Trench (36,069ft/10,994m deep)
COLDEST OCEAN: Arctic Ocean
WARMEST OCEAN: Indian Ocean
SALTIEST SEA: Dead Sea (33.7% salt)
LONGEST RIVER: Nile River (4132mi/6650km)
BIGGEST LAKE: Caspian Sea (143,244mi²/371,000km²)

15% OF THE WORLD'S OCEAN IS COVERED BY ICE, THOUGH WITH CLIMATE CHANGE, THIS PERCENTAGE IS GETTING SMALLER

SALTWATER CROCODILE

PUFFIN

POLAR BEAR

OCEANS PRODUCE 70% OF THE WORLD'S OXYGEN

CLOWNFISH

CORAL

DUGONG

FRIGATEBIRD

TRUMPETFISH

GIANT OARFISH

MORE PEOPLE HAVE BEEN TO OUTER SPACE THAN TO THE BOTTOM OF THE OCEAN!

NARWHAL

PUFFERFISH

HAMMERHEAD SHARK

LEAFY SEADRAGON

NAUTILUS

SOUTHERN RIGHT
60FT/18.3M

SEI
52.5FT/16M

SPERM
67FT/20.5M

HUMPBACK
52.5FT/16M

MINKE
34.5FT/10.5M

OUR SKY

ATMOSPHERE

Most other planets have atmospheres but Earth is the only planet in our solar system that can support plant and animal life (that we know of!). Earth's atmosphere is made up of 78 per cent nitrogen, 21 per cent oxygen, 0.9 per cent argon and 0.03 per cent carbon (with teensy scraps of other gases like helium and neon). There are different levels of atmosphere, thinning out as you go higher and higher. There is no atmosphere at all in deep space.

SOUTHERN ROYAL ALBATROSS

SHY ALBATROSS

GREATER SNOW GOOSE

93 MILLION MILES (150 MILLION KILOMETERS) FROM EARTH

HIGH FLYERS

Vultures, cranes, geese, swans, storks and condors are some of the highest-flying birds in the world. Rüppell's griffon vulture flies the highest, at over 36,000 feet (11,000 meters). That's as high as a plane! Other high-flyers include helicopters, hot air balloons and the highest of all ... spacecraft and satellites. The Northern Lights (Aurora Borealis) and Southern Lights (Aurora Australis) appear as high as 398 miles (640 kilometers) above the Earth's surface.

WHOOPER SWAN

OSPREY

BALD EAGLE

MONARCH BUTTERFLY

FRUIT BAT

ULYSSES BUTTERFLY

NATURE'S PILOTS

From backyard sparrows through to the highest-flying migratory birds that travel from one side of the world to the other, birds are the rulers of our skies. Other animals you'll see in the sky include insects and bats (the only mammal that can actually fly), as well as gliding fish, frogs, reptiles and mammals, like the sugar glider.

BLACK SWAN

TOCO TOUCAN

SCARLET MACAW

SUGAR GLIDER

BUMBLEBEE

WIND-POWERED

Wind power provides clean, renewable energy. Just one wind turbine can provide enough energy for a whole house. Windmills have been used for hundreds of years and you can see them all around the world – from farms to inner-city canals.

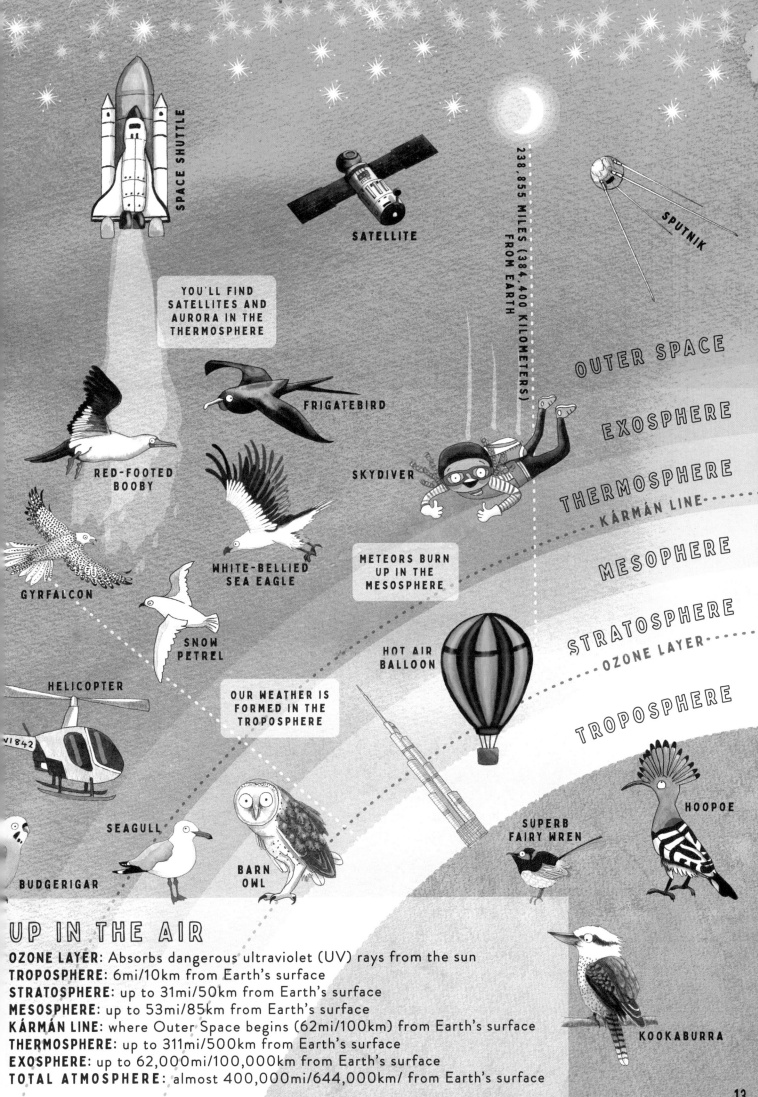

SPACE SHUTTLE

SATELLITE

238,855 MILES (384,400 KILOMETERS) FROM EARTH

SPUTNIK

YOU'LL FIND SATELLITES AND AURORA IN THE THERMOSPHERE

FRIGATEBIRD

OUTER SPACE

EXOSPHERE

SKYDIVER

THERMOSPHERE

KÁRMÁN LINE

RED-FOOTED BOOBY

GYRFALCON

WHITE-BELLIED SEA EAGLE

METEORS BURN UP IN THE MESOSPHERE

MESOSPHERE

SNOW PETREL

HOT AIR BALLOON

STRATOSPHERE

OZONE LAYER

HELICOPTER

V1842

OUR WEATHER IS FORMED IN THE TROPOSPHERE

TROPOSPHERE

HOOPOE

SEAGULL

BARN OWL

SUPERB FAIRY WREN

BUDGERIGAR

KOOKABURRA

UP IN THE AIR

OZONE LAYER: Absorbs dangerous ultraviolet (UV) rays from the sun
TROPOSPHERE: 6mi/10km from Earth's surface
STRATOSPHERE: up to 31mi/50km from Earth's surface
MESOSPHERE: up to 53mi/85km from Earth's surface
KÁRMÁN LINE: where Outer Space begins (62mi/100km) from Earth's surface
THERMOSPHERE: up to 311mi/500km from Earth's surface
EXOSPHERE: up to 62,000mi/100,000km from Earth's surface
TOTAL ATMOSPHERE: almost 400,000mi/644,000km/ from Earth's surface

EARTHLY EXTREMES

Our world is a place of extremes. Largest, smallest, coldest, hottest, fastest, slowest. Be amazed!

132 DECIBELS IS AS LOUD AS A GUN!

QUIETEST BIRD
OWL Fringed feathers make for silent flight

LOUDEST BIRD
KAKAPO At 132 decibels, it can be heard 4.4mi/7km away!

SMALLEST BIRD
HUMMINGBIRD 2.2in/5.7cm

THE RUBY-THROATED HUMMINGBIRD BEATS ITS WINGS 200 TIMES PER SECOND!

BIGGEST BIRD
OSTRICH up to 9ft/2.8m

HIGHEST CLOUDS
CIRRUS over 9mi/15km

CIRRUS

LOWEST CLOUDS
STRATUS AND CUMULUS below 6562ft/2000m

STRATUS

CUMULUS

SMALLEST MOUNTAIN
MOUNT WYCHEPROOF 486ft/148m

TALLEST MOUNTAIN
MOUNT EVEREST 29,029ft/8848m

SIZE AGAINST EVEREST

TALLEST BUILDING
BURJ KHALIFA 2722ft/829.8m

SMALLEST BUILDING
WORLD'S LITTLEST SKYSCRAPER 39ft/12m

HIGHEST POINT
MOUNT EVEREST 29,029ft/8848m

SMALLEST COUNTRY
VATICAN CITY 0.17mi²/0.44km²

LARGEST COUNTRY
RUSSIA 6.6 million mi²/ 17.1 million km²

SMALLEST CITY
VATICAN CITY 800 people

TOO SMALL TO SHOW HERE!

SMALLEST TREE
DWARF WILLOW up to 2.2in/6cm high

BIGGEST TREE
GIANT REDWOOD 380ft/115.7m high

THE WORLD'S TALLEST TREE HAS BEEN NICKNAMED HYPERION WHICH MEANS 'HIGH ONE'

MOST PEOPLE
ASIA almost 4.5 billion people

LEAST PEOPLE
ANTARCTICA about 4000 people visit every year

CHALLENGER DEEP, MARIANA TRENCH -35,814ft/-10,916m

SUNNIEST CITY
YUMA, USA
4015 hours per year

RAINIEST CITY
MAWSYNRAM, INDIA
467in/11,871mm per year

VS

BUSIEST PLACE
MONG KOK DISTRICT,
HONG KONG

VS

QUIETEST PLACE
ZURICH,
SWITZERLAND

ZURICH HAS THE
LOWEST NOISE
POLLUTION OF
ALL CITIES
ON EARTH

BIGGEST CITY
TOKYO, JAPAN
37.4 million people

SALAR DE UYUNI IS
THE LARGEST SALT
LAKE ON EARTH AT
4085MI²/10,582KM²

FLATTEST
SALAR DE UYUNI,
BOLIVIA

VS

MOST MOUNTAINOUS
BHUTAN

THE LAND OF
BHUTAN IS
98.8%
MOUNTAINS

MOST NORTHERN CITY
NY-ÅLESUND, NORWAY
78°55'30"N

VS

MOST SOUTHERN CITY
USHUAIA, ARGENTINA
54°48'7"S

FASTEST ANIMAL
CHEETAH up to 75mi/120km per hour

VS

SLOWEST ANIMAL
SLOTH 0.15mi/0.24km per hour

SIZE
AGAINST
WHALE

LARGEST MARINE ANIMAL
BLUE WHALE 98.4ft/30m

VS

LARGEST LAND ANIMAL
AFRICAN ELEPHANT 10.8ft/3.3m

THE SMALLEST
ANIMALS OF ALL
ARE BACTERIA:
MUCH TOO SMALL
TO SEE HERE!

HOTTEST COUNTRY
MALI 82.85°F/28.25°C average

VS

COLDEST COUNTRY
CANADA 22.37°F/-5.35°C average

HOTTEST
TEMPERATURE
DEATH VALLEY,
USA, 1913

134°F
56.7°C

VS

COLDEST
TEMPERATURE
VOSTOK STATION,
ANTARCTICA, 1983

-128.6°F
-89.2°C

15

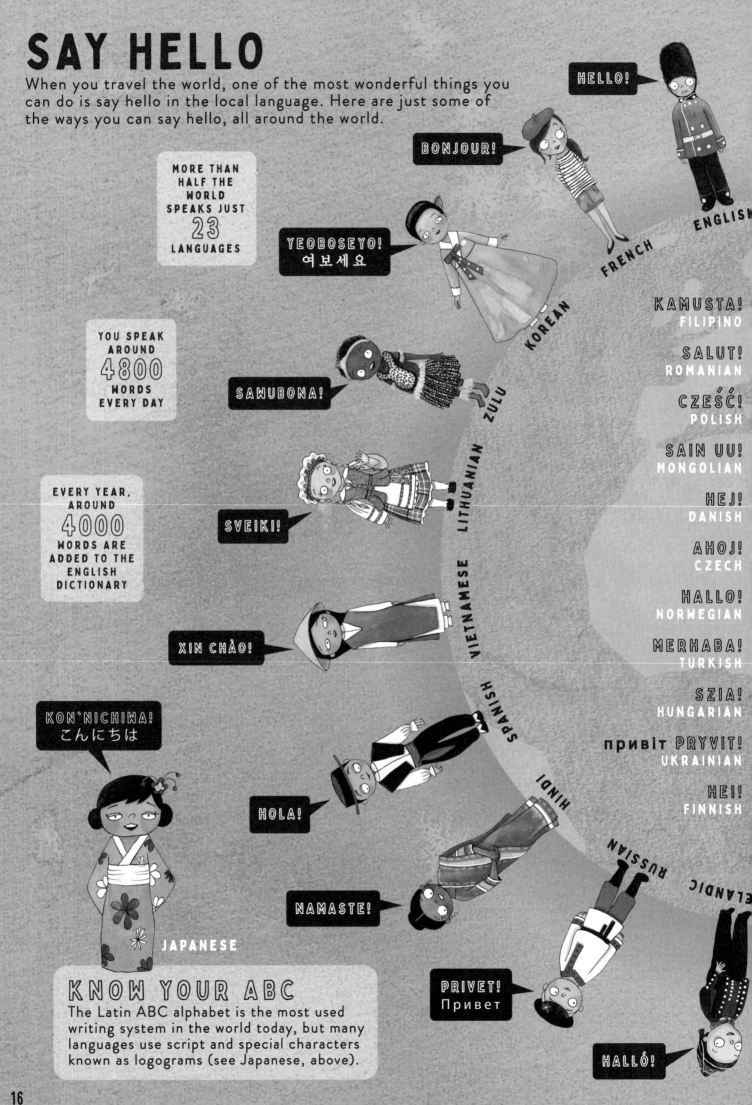

SAY HELLO

When you travel the world, one of the most wonderful things you can do is say hello in the local language. Here are just some of the ways you can say hello, all around the world.

HELLO!
ENGLISH

BONJOUR!
FRENCH

MORE THAN HALF THE WORLD SPEAKS JUST 23 LANGUAGES

YEOBOSEYO!
여보세요
KOREAN

KAMUSTA!
FILIPINO

SALUT!
ROMANIAN

CZEŚĆ!
POLISH

SAIN UU!
MONGOLIAN

YOU SPEAK AROUND 4800 WORDS EVERY DAY

SAWUBONA!
ZULU

HEJ!
DANISH

AHOJ!
CZECH

LITHUANIAN

SVEIKI!

EVERY YEAR, AROUND 4000 WORDS ARE ADDED TO THE ENGLISH DICTIONARY

HALLO!
NORWEGIAN

MERHABA!
TURKISH

VIETNAMESE

XIN CHÀO!

SZIA!
HUNGARIAN

привіт PRYVIT!
UKRAINIAN

SPANISH

HEI!
FINNISH

KON'NICHIWA!
こんにちは

HOLA!

HINDI

NAMASTE!

RUSSIAN

ICELANDIC

JAPANESE

KNOW YOUR ABC

The Latin ABC alphabet is the most used writing system in the world today, but many languages use script and special characters known as logograms (see Japanese, above).

PRIVET!
Привет

HALLÓ!

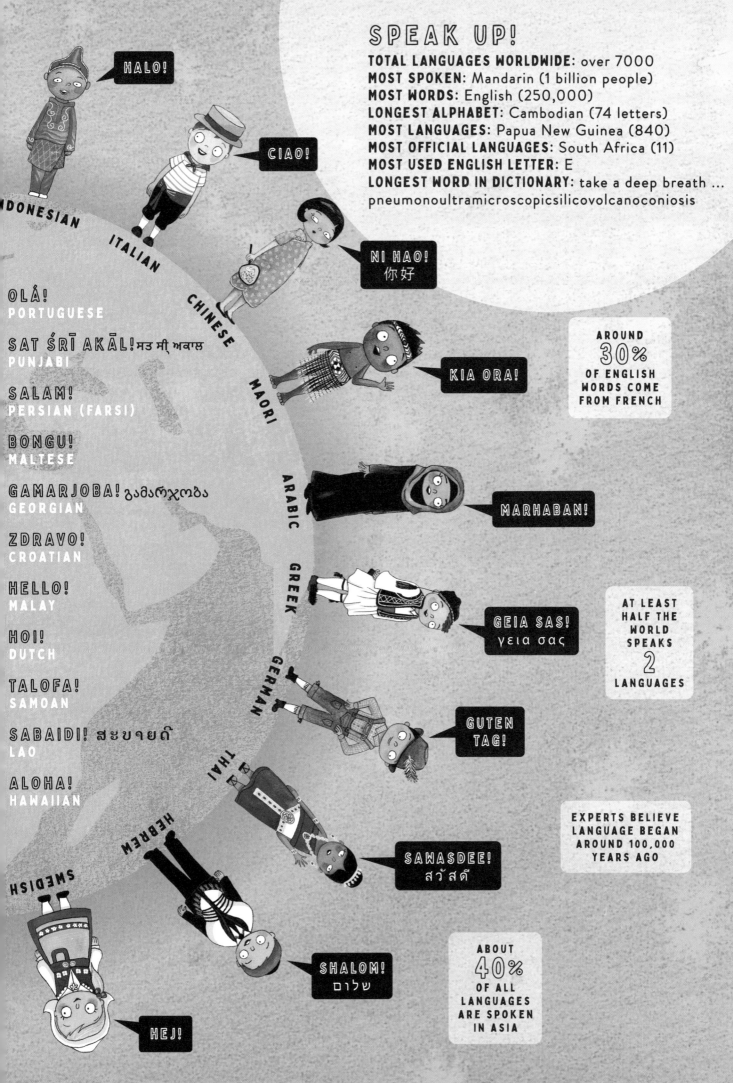

RAINBOW PLANET

From the pink blossoms of Japan to purple grapes in Italy, the world is a gelato treat of color. But the same color can represent many different things, and meanings change depending on where you live!

RAINBOW LORIKEET

TRAVELLER'S PALM

FOUR-LEAF CLOVER

BEETROOT

RED ROBIN

CHERRIES

CHERRY BLOSSOM

MAPLE LEAF

RED FOX

ANGELFISH

GREENBACK FLOUNDER

CORAL

BUDGERIGAR

KIWI FRUIT

ULURU

CLOWNFISH

MONARCH BUTTERFLY

CHINESE DRAGON

YELLOW KAPOK

CORN

STATUE OF LIBERTY

ORANGE

Orange is the color of the Dutch royal family. For Hindus, it's a sacred color, and Buddhist monks often wear orange robes. Orange is the only main color to be named after an object – the juicy orange.

RASPBERRY

LEAFY SEADRAGON

KIRUNA KYRKA

SANTA CLAUS

CHEESE

PALM

GREEN

Nature's primary color, green means life, growth and nature, as well as luck and wisdom. It can also represent money, jealousy and evil! It's a sacred color for Muslims, meaning strength.

ORANGE

HONEY ANT

BUMBLEBEE

RED

Red and pink mean love – think Valentine's Day! For Indigenous Australians, red is a ceremonial color. In Asia, it means good fortune, happiness and wealth. Red can also mean courage, anger and even danger!

MANGO

YELLOW

Yellow is the color of creativity and happiness, courage and bravery, but it can also mean you're a coward! The emperors of China wore yellow. In Greece, it means sadness, while in Germany and France, it's the color of jealousy.

MELBOURNE TRAM

PEAR

ORANGUTAN

CLOUDBERRIES

RUBY

GREEN TREE FROG

POMEGRANATE

FLAMINGO

BENGAL TIGER

HONEY

LEMON GELATO

GOLD

EMERALD

GRAPES

LOCH NESS MONSTER

ULYSSES BUTTERFLY

BLUE JAY

TABRIZ BLUE MOSQUE

SUPERB FAIRY WREN

BLUE

Blue can mean calm, freedom, trust, peace and security. It can also mean you're lonely or sad. In Korea, dark blue is the color of grief. For Hindus, it means joy. In the Middle East, it represents heaven, and in Greece and Turkey, it protects against the evil eye.

BURJ KHALIFA

MING VASE

BLUE SWIMMER CRAB

SAPPHIRE

BLUE WHALE

PEACOCK

SAFFRON CROCUS

FIGS

AMETHYST

ROYAL BLUEBELL

STARFISH

THISTLE

MULLA MULLA

PURPLE

Purple is the color of kings and queens, wealth and power. It often represents faith and spirituality. In Thailand and Brazil, it's the color of grief. In the USA, it means courage and strength. The Purple Heart medal is awarded to the bravest of soldiers.

URCHIN

CORAL

JACARANDA

LAVENDER

GRAPES

PASSIFLORA

CHURROS

SHELL

GRIZZLY BEAR

BROWN

Brown is seen as simple, stable, earthy, supportive, honest and strong. It can also mean health. In the Middle East, it represents comfort, and in Asia, it's the color of grief.

MOOSE

COMMON WOMBAT

SUGAR SHACK

FUR SEAL

BEAVER

FRUIT BAT

ECHIDNA

SAGRADA FAMILIA

PLATYPUS

COCONUT

PILOT FISH

BLACK WIDOW SPIDER

AFRICAN PENGUIN

ZEBRA

BLACK SWAN

ORCA

COAL

MOAI STATUES

BLACK

Black means many things including strength, mystery, grief, elegance, magic and bad luck! In some African countries, it represents age and wisdom. For Muslims, it means rebirth.

SPANISH FIGHTING BULL

IT'S A PARADE!

For many thousands of years, people have developed clothing styles and national costumes to suit their climate, the daily weather and their way of life. Some are casual and some are all dressed up. Some are highly decorated and some are plain. From Arctic coats thick with fur to Indian silk saris, here are just some of the traditional costumes and clothing found all around the world.

SOUTH AFRICA

INDIA

GERMANY

JAPAN

ICELAND

ARGENTINA

HUNGARY

VIETNAM

MEXICO

SPAIN

ETHIOPIA

SWEDEN

TAHITI

GREECE

THE

AUSTRALIA

ITALY

NIGERIA

KOREA

IRAQ

LITHUANIA

NEW ZEALAND

FRANCE

SWITZERLAND

CANADA

CHINA

EGYPT

UKRAINE

RUSSIA

ISRAEL

THAILAND

BUILD IT UP

From ancient creations and carved temples made of stone, to towering skyscrapers made of glass and steel, here are just some of the beautiful buildings and monuments found all over the world. Today, UNESCO gives some structures a World Heritage Site status, to ensure they are well cared for.

SAGRADA FAMILIA Spain
Designed by architect Antoni Gaudi, work began on this beautiful church in 1882. And it's still being built! When complete, it will have 18 towers.

SYDNEY OPERA HOUSE Australia
Perched on the edge of Sydney Harbour, this opera house has over one million roof tiles, all made in Sweden. The building is cooled by water taken straight from the harbour.

STATUE OF LIBERTY USA
A gift from France, this copper statue is an icon of freedom. Lady Liberty stands 305 feet (93 meters) high. Her torch is covered in sheets of gold and the seven points on her crown represent the seven continents.

HAGIA SOPHIA Turkey
This magnificent building was once a church then a mosque. It's now a museum and has the second-largest dome in the world. Almost 1500 years old, it only took six years to build!

THE LITTLE MERMAID Denmark
Made of bronze and granite, this statue was made in 1913 and was inspired by Hans Christian Andersen's fairy tale *The Little Mermaid.*

FORBIDDEN CITY China
The world's largest imperial palace, the Forbidden City has 980 buildings. Finished in 1420 by one million workers, it was home to 24 Chinese emperors.

BURJ KHALIFA United Arab Emirates
Completed in 2009, the world's tallest building stands an astonishing 2722 feet (829.8 meters) high. The elevator to the observation deck is super fast. It only takes one minute to fly up 124 floors!

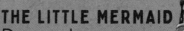

KIRUNA KYRKA Sweden
This church is one of Sweden's largest wooden buildings. It was built to look like a Laplander's tent, and was voted the country's most beloved building!

WESTMINSTER UK
The Palace of Westminster was once a royal palace and is now home to the Houses of Parliament. It's been destroyed by fire and rebuilt not once, but twice. The bell inside the tower is called Big Ben.

PYRAMIDS OF GIZA Egypt
Built around 4500 years ago, these pyramids were built as tombs for the kings of Egypt. The largest pyramid is made of 2.3 million stone bricks.

TAJ MAHAL India
The 'crown of palaces' was built in memory of an emperor's wife. Made of white marble and precious stones, it was built by 22,000 people. Around 1000 elephants were used to carry building materials.

ANGKOR Cambodia
An ancient site of sandstone temples, Angkor (meaning city of temples) is around 900 years old and covers an amazing 154 square miles (400 square kilometers).

ACROPOLIS Greece
Made of limestone rock as old as the dinosaurs, the Acropolis is an ancient site of four hills. Built over 2460 years ago, the Parthenon is a temple dedicated to the goddess Athena.

WINDMILLS The Netherlands
There are over 1000 windmills left in Holland. They are used for many things, from grinding grain to draining water and making paper.

EIFFEL TOWER France
Made of iron, the Eiffel Tower is one of the world's most beloved monuments. It stands 1050 feet (320 meters) high and was the tallest structure in the world for 41 years (from 1889). In summer, the tower grows by 6 inches (15 centimeters), as the metal expands in the heat!

COLOSSEUM Italy
Tens of thousands of slaves were used to build the Colosseum, finished in 80AD. It's so big, an entire football field can fit inside! Roman games and festivals were held here, sometimes lasting 100 days.

PORT ARTHUR Australia
This historic site and penal colony was built by the convicts sent to Australia from England. The prison closed in 1877.

PETRONAS TOWERS Malaysia
At 1483 feet (452 metres), the double-decker skybridge between the towers is the world's highest. Covered in thousands of glass panels, each tower weighs 330,000 tons (300,000 tonnes)!

STONEHENGE UK
Made up of enormous stones and burial pits, it took over 1000 years to build this sacred site. Work first began around 5000 years ago.

GOLDEN GATE BRIDGE USA
The Golden Gate is 1 mile (1.6 kilometres) long and was once the longest and tallest bridge in the world. Its bright color is called international orange. It makes the bridge stand out on a typical foggy San Francisco day.

KEMI SNOW HOTEL Finland
Just like an igloo, this snow hotel is temporary. It's rebuilt each winter, with a new floor plan each time. Guests are given fur blankets and Arctic sleeping bags, and at 23°F/-5°C inside the hotel, they need them!

PETRA Jordan
Carved into red sandstone, Petra was founded in 312BC and is one of the oldest cities ever built. It had a water system that made lush gardens bloom in the desert!

MOAI Easter Island
These ancient statues were first carved by the Rapa Nui people around 900 years ago. There are 887 in total. Most of the Moai statues also have bodies, which have become buried over time.

ST BASIL'S CATHEDRAL Russia
Brightly colored, with onion-shaped domes, St Basil's was built by the first tsar of Russia, Ivan the Terrible. It was finished in 1561. The cathedral is actually nine churches in one! Today, it's a museum.

THE WHITE HOUSE USA
This huge mansion has six floors, 132 rooms and 35 bathrooms! George Washington is the only president who never lived in the White House. President Roosevelt came up with its name in 1901.

CHICHÉN ITZÁ Mexico
This sacred city was built by the Mayan people over 1400 years ago. The Pyramid 'El Castillo' (The Castle) is one of the New Seven Wonders of the World.

FOOD, GLORIOUS FOOD!

Gobble your way around the world with this banquet of scrumptious eats. Fruit and vegetables, the sweetest of treats, and national dishes – from Poland to Peru! Enjoy choc-dipped churros in Spain, slippery noodles in Japan or honey ants in Australia. Part of the joy of travel is sampling new foods!

FAMOUS DISHES

DUMPLINGS

Dumplings are made all over the world but the Chinese dumpling may be the most famous of all. Plump with meat and vegetables, it can be steamed or fried.

SAUSAGE
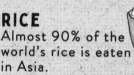
Germany is famous for its sausages, with bratwurst being one of the most popular kinds. There are around 1500 types of German sausage!

RICE

Almost 90% of the world's rice is eaten in Asia.

KEBAB

Many countries have their own types of grilled meat kebab. This Turkish shish kebab is grilled with tomato and green bell pepper.

SUSHI

Would you eat raw fish and sticky rice wrapped in seaweed? Sushi is hugely popular today but it was first made in Japan around 1200 years ago!

PIEROGI
Pierogi are a type of Polish dumpling. They have both sweet and savory fillings.

PIE
Stuffed with vegetables, meat, fruits and custards, pies are loved all over the world. The first pies were made from pastry that wasn't meant to be eaten. It was just a container for the filling!

RUISLEIPÄ
This dark, sour rye is the most popular bread in Finland. It can last for months without spoiling.

BUSH TUCKER

The finger lime, honey ant and witchetty grub are types of food Indigenous Australians call 'bush tucker'. All around the world, Indigenous people enjoy foods plucked right from the land. This is sometimes called foraging.

NOODLES

The first noodles came from China over 4000 years ago. Since then, many countries have adopted the noodle. Popular types include rice, udon, ramen, glass, egg and spaghetti!

PIZZA
Pizza was first cooked up in Naples, Italy. The famous margherita pizza was made for Queen Margherita in 1889. It was topped with tomatoes, mozzarella cheese and basil, just like it is today!

PAVLOVA

Who invented this delicious meringue and cream dessert? Australians and New Zealande continue to battle it out!

COFFEE OR TEA?

A percolated coffee in the USA or a caffè lattè in Italy? A matcha green tea in Japan or a milky tea in England? A thick, sticky coffee in Turkey or tea boiled in a traditional samovar in Russia? If you visit Russia, don't forget a sweet treat with your tea.

RUSSIAN SAMOVAR

JAPANESE MATCHA TEA

TURKISH COFFEE

ITALIAN CAFFE LATTE

AMERICAN BLACK COFFEE

VIETNAMESE COFFEE

ENGLISH TEA WITH MILK

TUTTI FRUTTI

Coconuts from the Pacific Islands, kiwi fruit from New Zealand, apples from Poland, bananas from Ecuador and lingonberries from Sweden. It's the world inside your fruit bowl!

SERBIAN RASPBERRIES

SWEDISH LINGONBERRIES

SWEDISH CLOUDBERRIES

INDONESIAN GOOSEBERRIES

AMERICAN CRANBERRIES

SWEET TREATS

Our global sweet shop is bursting with delicious cakes, slices, cookies, ice creams, pastries and nature's bounty, like honey and maple syrup.

ITALIAN GELATO

JAPANESE MOCHI

SPANISH CHURROS

GREEK BAKLAVA

FRENCH MACARON

AUSTRALIAN LAMINGTON

ITALIAN TARTUFO

TURKISH DELIGHT

UKRAINIAN HONEY

CANADIAN MAPLE SYRUP

AMERICAN DONUT

EVERYDAY STAPLES

Many of the foods you eat every day are grown or produced all around the world. Have you tried olive oil from Greece, potatoes from Peru, avocados from Mexico or pasta from Italy? There are endless types of bread worldwide, but history tells us it was first made in the Middle East.

SWISS CHEESE

FRENCH BRIE

IRISH BUTTER

ITALIAN PASTA

GREEK OLIVE OIL

AMERICAN SOURDOUGH

VEG OUT

DUTCH TOMATOES

MEXICAN AVOCADOS AND CHILLIES

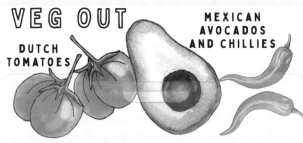

PERUVIAN POTATOES

RUSSIAN BEETS

HOME, SWEET HOME

From underground burrows to mobile homes and the rise of the teensy tiny house, there are countless types of houses around the world. Here is a peek at just some of the world's homes, built to cope with climate conditions or landscapes, from steep mountainsides to swamps.

CAVES
The very first homes were made in caves where people could keep warm and dry and away from danger. People still live in cave homes, built into the mountainsides in Cappadocia in Turkey, or into the desert floor in Coober Pedy in Australia.

TENTS
People use yurts, wigwams, lavvus and tepees to move with the seasons or follow their animal herds. Indigenous Australians and the Sami people of Lapland made lean-tos and tents with animal hides.

MUD HOUSES
Over many thousands of years, houses have been made from the earth. From the Chinese tulou to the mud towers of Togo in Africa, these houses can be built with bricks, wood and tin sheets.

HUTS
Huts are super simple houses made of stone, wood, leaves, ice and whatever people can get their hands on! There's the African rondavel, the Arctic igloo and the Indonesian honai. In west Africa, cattle farmers make temporary huts from woven reeds.

WOODEN HOUSES
There are many types of wooden house, from izba log cabins in Russia and painted houses in Finland, to outback homesteads in Australia and turf houses built into the ground in Iceland.

STILT HOUSES
Stilt houses lift homes above water, like pang uk houses in Hong Kong, eucalyptus wood houses in Ecuador, Khmer houses in Cambodia. Stilts can raise houses up to catch cooling breezes, like the Australian Queenslander house.

ECO-HOUSES
Eco-houses are friendly to the environment. They use recycled or sustainable materials and are built to use far less energy, or to use planet-friendly renewable energy, like solar panels.

TINY HOUSES
As the world's population grows and grows, the teensy tiny house has become very popular. In Japan, people live in the tiniest of homes because there's not a lot of space. Tiny homes are cheaper to run and are good for our planet.

TINY HOUSE
CANADA

HOUSE
The free-standing house is one of the most common types of homes. It can be made of all sorts of things, including wood, glass, bricks, stone, cement or even haybales. Types include cottage, bungalow, mansion and ranch.

TERRACE HOUSE
Also called townhouses or row houses, these narrow homes are joined together. They're often found in cities like London or Amsterdam.

COMMON

APARTMENT
Also called a flat or unit, an apartment might be snug to the ground or skyscraper high. Today, many cities, like Hong Kong or New York, are packed with apartments, but the first apartments were actually built 2000 years ago by the Ancient Romans!

RONDAVEL
SOUTH AFRICA

WOVEN REEDS
WEST AFRICA

TENTS ARE
TEMPORARY
HOMES THAT CAN
BE PACKED UP
AND MOVED FROM
PLACE TO PLACE

TENTS

TEPEE
NORTH
AMERICA

LAVVU
SCANDINAVIA

HUTS

IGLOO
ARCTIC
CIRCLE

HONAI
INDONESIA

MUD BRICK AND TIN
AFRICA

YURT
MONGOLIA

THE IGLOO IS
A TEMPORARY
HOUSE. WHEN THE
WEATHER WARMS,
IT MELTS!

MUD TOWERS
TOGO

MUD

MUD HOUSES ARE
CHEAP TO MAKE
AND CAN PROTECT
FAMILIES FROM
THE HOT SUN

HOMESTEAD
AUSTRALIA

TULOU
CHINA

KHMER
CAMBODIA

QUEENSLANDER
AUSTRALIA

ROW HOUSES
FINLAND

MANY HOUSES
IN FINLAND ARE
PAINTED A
TRADITIONAL
COLOR CALLED
FALUN RED

STILT

WOODEN

IZBA LOG CABIN
RUSSIA

STILT HOUSE
ECUADOR

IN THE ARCTIC
CIRCLE, STILTS
RAISE HOUSES
UP OFF THE
FREEZING
GROUND

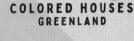

COLORED HOUSES
GREENLAND

TURF HOUSE
ICELAND

TREEHOUSE
DENMARK

HOUSEBOAT
GERMANY

LIGHTHOUSE
IRELAND

UNIQUE

CASTLE
SCOTLAND

**SHIPPING
CONTAINERS**
THAILAND

WOULD YOU LIVE HERE?

Would you live in a lighthouse? A castle? What about a treehouse or a houseboat? A metal shipping container?
As housing gets more and more expensive, people look for ways to turn old buildings into homes or re-use
items (like shipping containers!) that might be thrown away. The results are some pretty cool places to live.

BOUNTIFUL BLOOMS

There are around 260,000 types of flowering plants, covering all seven continents – even Antarctica! Found everywhere from the top of a tree (jacaranda) to the bottom of the ocean (seagrass), flowers are Mother Nature's most beautiful accessory. They're also used in so very many ways, from perfume to food!

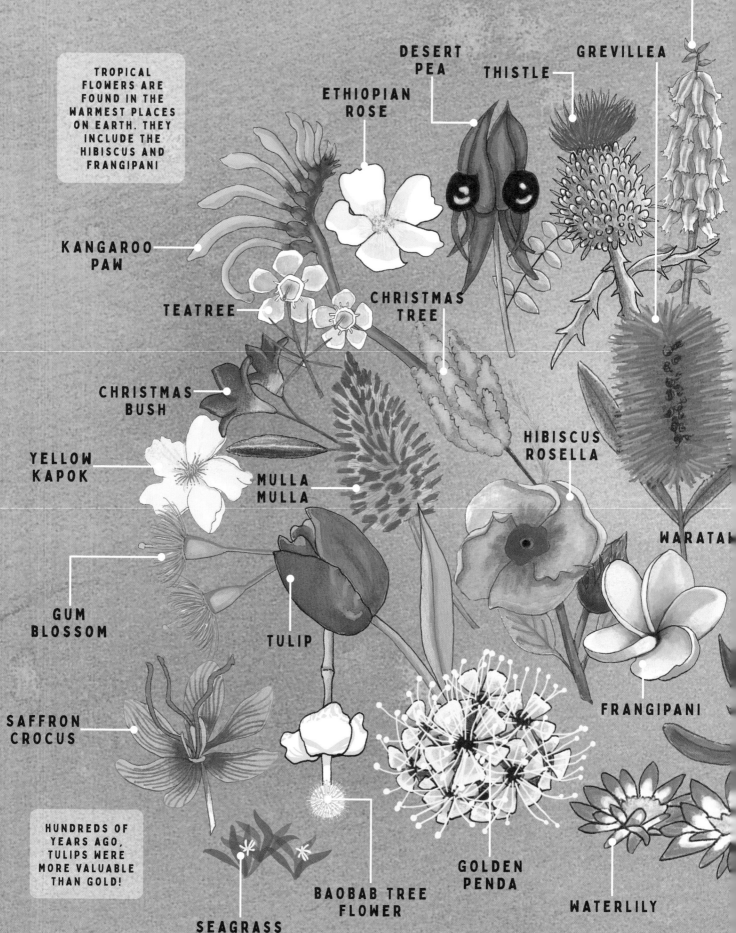

TROPICAL FLOWERS ARE FOUND IN THE WARMEST PLACES ON EARTH. THEY INCLUDE THE HIBISCUS AND FRANGIPANI

COMMON HEATH

DESERT PEA

THISTLE

GREVILLEA

ETHIOPIAN ROSE

KANGAROO PAW

TEATREE

CHRISTMAS TREE

CHRISTMAS BUSH

HIBISCUS ROSELLA

YELLOW KAPOK

MULLA MULLA

WARATAH

GUM BLOSSOM

TULIP

FRANGIPANI

SAFFRON CROCUS

HUNDREDS OF YEARS AGO, TULIPS WERE MORE VALUABLE THAN GOLD!

GOLDEN PENDA

WATERLILY

SEAGRASS

BAOBAB TREE FLOWER

LAVENDER

HELICONIA

CHERRY
BLOSSOM

LEAFLESS
ORCHID

GOLDEN
WATTLE

FLOWERS
FIRST APPEARED
BETWEEN 250
AND 140 MILLION
YEARS AGO!

BROCCOLI
IS ACTUALLY
A FLOWER!

STURT'S
DESERT
ROSE

COOKTOWN
ORCHID

POINCIANA

STAR
FLOWER

ROYAL
BLUEBELL

FLANNEL
FLOWER

PASSIFLORA

BANKSIA

STICKY
KURRAJONG

EARTH IS DIVIDED
INTO NINE BOTANICAL
CONTINENTS — EUROPE,
AFRICA, ASIA TEMPERATE,
ASIA TROPICAL, PACIFIC,
AUSTRALASIA, NORTHERN
AMERICA, SOUTHERN
AMERICA AND
ANTARCTICA

PROTEA

MEXICAN
DAISY

JACARANDA

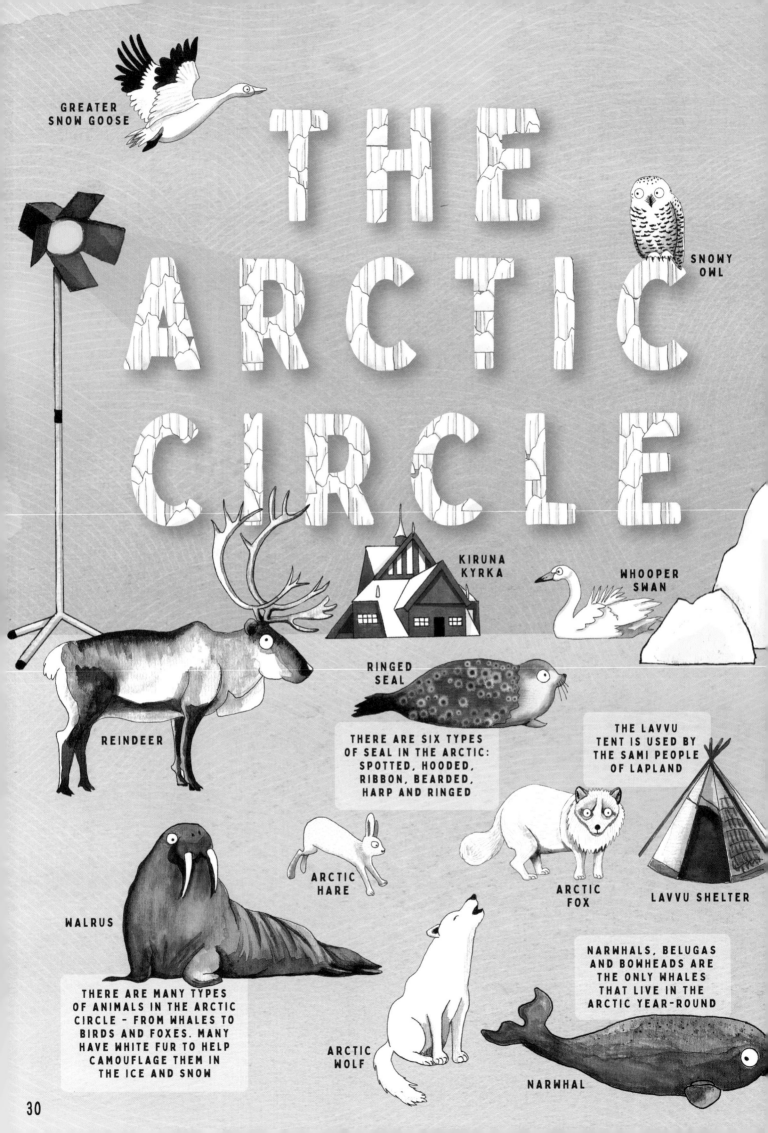

GREATER
SNOW GOOSE

THE ARCTIC CIRCLE

SNOWY
OWL

KIRUNA
KYRKA

WHOOPER
SWAN

REINDEER

RINGED
SEAL

THERE ARE SIX TYPES
OF SEAL IN THE ARCTIC:
SPOTTED, HOODED,
RIBBON, BEARDED,
HARP AND RINGED

THE LAVVU
TENT IS USED BY
THE SAMI PEOPLE
OF LAPLAND

ARCTIC
HARE

ARCTIC
FOX

LAVVU SHELTER

WALRUS

NARWHALS, BELUGAS
AND BOWHEADS ARE
THE ONLY WHALES
THAT LIVE IN THE
ARCTIC YEAR-ROUND

THERE ARE MANY TYPES
OF ANIMALS IN THE ARCTIC
CIRCLE - FROM WHALES TO
BIRDS AND FOXES. MANY
HAVE WHITE FUR TO HELP
CAMOUFLAGE THEM IN
THE ICE AND SNOW

ARCTIC
WOLF

NARWHAL

THE ICY NORTH POLE

The Arctic Circle sits at the tippety-top of our planet, and cuts through eight countries – Russia, Norway, Sweden, Finland, Greenland, the United States, Canada and Iceland. You may see Santa Claus at the North Pole but you'll see no trees! Plants can be found, but they're limited to mosses, grasses and lichens. Because of the way the Earth tilts, the Arctic Circle receives 163 days of total darkness each year, and the midnight sun stays in the sky for 187 days!

AREA: 7.7 million mi²/20 million km²
NAME: Arctic comes from the Greek arktos, meaning bear (the pole star Ursa Major sits in the Great Bear constellation)
MAIN LANGUAGES: Russian, English, Scandinavian languages
POPULATION: 4 million (2019)
LARGEST CITY: Murmansk, Russia (307,000 people)
HIGHEST POINT: Gunnbjørn Fjeld, Greenland (12,119ft/3694m)
LOWEST POINT: Arctic Ocean (sea level)

PUFFIN

ERMINE

THE AURORA BOREALIS (NORTHERN LIGHTS) IS A SPECTACULAR, NATURAL LIGHT SHOW OF SWIRLING COLOR AGAINST THE NIGHT SKY. THE BEST TIME TO SEE THE LIGHTS IS FROM SEPTEMBER TO MARCH

THERE ARE POLAR STATIONS AND METEOROLOGICAL CENTERS IN THE ARCTIC CIRCLE, BUT MODERN CITIES AND HOTELS, TOO

KEMI SNOW HOTEL

IGLOO COMES FROM AN INUIT WORD MEANING HOME. WHEN IT'S FREEZING OUTSIDE, THE IGLOO IS SNUG AND DRY

IGLOO

SANTA CLAUS

ELK

THE POLAR BEAR HAS BLACK SKIN! ITS FUR IS ACTUALLY TRANSPARENT BUT IT LOOKS WHITE BECAUSE OF THE WAY IT REFLECTS LIGHT

ICELANDIC SHEEP WERE FIRST BROUGHT TO ICELAND BY THE VIKINGS

ICELANDIC SHEEP

POLAR BEAR

BELUGA WHALE

IT'S ALL IN THE DETAILS...

COUNTRIES: 23
AREA: 9.5 million mi²/24.7 million km²
LARGEST COUNTRY: Canada (3.8 million mi²/9.9 million km²)
SMALLEST COUNTRY: Saint Kitts and Nevis (100mi²/261km²)
NAME: America was named after Italian explorer Amerigo Vespucci (1454–1512)
MAJOR LANGUAGES: English, Spanish, French, Creole, native languages and dialects
POPULATION: 366 million (2019)
LARGEST CITY: Mexico City, Mexico (20.9 million)
HIGHEST POINT: Denali, Alaska (20,308ft/6190m)
LOWEST POINT: Death Valley (282ft/86m below sea level)
LONGEST RIVER: Mississippi River (2347mi/3778km)
BIGGEST LAKE: Lake Superior (31,700mi²/82,103km²)

AWESOME FAUNA

Canada, the USA and Mexico have a huge range of fauna – from spider monkeys in Mexico to polar bears in Canada. Here are just some of the amazing creatures you'll find from the tropics all the way up to the Arctic Circle.

MEXICAN SPIDER MONKEY
The Mexican spider monkey spends most of its time flying through the trees, holding on with its prehensile (gripping) tail. Sadly, this monkey is critically endangered.

SMALL BEASTS

RACCOON
The raccoon is a clean freak – it often washes its food in streams. It has some of the most humanlike hands of all animals. Its black 'mask' helps it see better at night.

COYOTE
Part of the dog family, the coyote will eat almost anything. It forms strong family groups called packs and is well-known for howling at the moon!

STRIPED SKUNK
The skunk is a slow mover. Because it can't outrun predators, it instead sprays them with a disgusting scent! This spray comes from two little glands under its tail. It smells like rotten eggs.

PORCUPINE
The porcupine may look cute and fluffy but the prickly quills on its back, sides and tail are far from cute! In Latin, porcupine means quill pig. It has orange teeth, like the beaver.

TEXAS LONGHORN
Both the males and females of this cattle breed have horns, which are actually part of the animal's skull. The longest recorded horns were 8.9 feet (2.7 meters) wide! Longhorns are very hardy. If there's no grass, they'll eat weeds and even cacti.

BIG CATS

JAGUAR
The jaguar is the largest cat in the Americas, and the third largest in the world, with a body up to about 6.5 feet (2 meters) long. It loves fish, and will use its own tail as a fishing line!

COUGAR
The cougar is a big, powerful cat – it can leap 39 feet (12 meters). It doesn't roar. Instead it either purrs like a kitten or screams like a human!

OCELOT
The ocelot is about twice the size of a house cat. Found in the USA and Mexico, the ocelot also can't roar.

BLUE JAY

The blue jay isn't really blue. Its feathers are made in such a way to make it look blue. The blue jay uses ants to groom its feathers, much like a comb!

NORTHERN CARDINAL

The cardinal is so popular, it's the state bird of seven states of the USA. Only the male is red.

BALD EAGLE

The bald eagle is the national animal of the USA. It's quite a cheeky bird – much of its food is stolen from other animals.

FLIGHT DECK

QUETZAL

The quetzal is one of the world's most beautiful birds. The male grows tail feathers almost twice as long as his body.

BEEP BEEP!

GREATER ROADRUNNER

The greater roadrunner can sprint at around 20 miles (32 kilometers) per hour. It loves to eat rattlesnakes!

QUARTER HORSE

The quarter horse is super fast over short distances, and that's where its name comes from ... it can beat most other horse breeds across a quarter mile (0.4 kilometres).

The pileated woodpecker can make such large holes, small trees can break in half!

PILEATED WOODPECKER

BIG BEASTS

BISON

The bison is the largest land animal in North America, and the national animal of the USA. Bulls can weigh up to 2204 pounds (1000 kilograms) and can run at over 34 miles (55 kilometers) per hour. The bison's hump is made of muscle.

GRIZZLY BEAR

The grizzly loves its food. It will eat almost anything and one of its favorite foods is moths. During hibernation, it can go without food and water for over 100 days. A grizzly's claws can be up to 4 inches (10 centimeters) long, so don't get too close!

35

CREATURES OF THE FAR NORTH

Many North American animals move between the USA and Canada, but many rely solely on the snowy and even Arctic conditions further north. Here are some of the creatures that roam in Canada.

GREAT MIGRATIONS

WHOOPING CRANE
This beautiful bird with long black legs and a red patch on its head is the tallest in North America (up to 5.2 feet/1.6 meters). It is endangered, with only 600 birds left in the wild.

GRAY WOLF
Gray wolves are very social. They communicate by barking, growling, howling and even dancing. Wolves are the largest member of the dog family.

CANADA GOOSE
When migrating, the Canada goose can cover an incredible 1490 miles (2400 kilometers) each day. These geese fly in a V-shape, and take turns flying in front.

FURRY CRITTERS

LITTLE RED FOX
This fox has amazing hearing – it can even hear creatures underground! Not all red foxes are red. Some are brown, black or silver. Its bushy tail can be used as a blanket to keep warm.

CANADA LYNX
This member of the cat family has huge paws that act as snowshoes in thick snow! It will often bury its prey in the snow to keep for later.

GROUNDHOG
The groundhog's teeth grow very fast – 0.05 inches (1.5 millimetres) every week! It digs underground mazes with several levels. On Groundhog Day in the USA, if a groundhog sees its shadow, there will be six more weeks of winter!

ELK

MOOSE

REINDEER

BEAVER
The beaver is always busy building. Its teeth look orange thanks to iron deposits that help keep the tooth enamel strong.

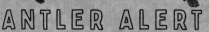

ANTLER ALERT
The reindeer, caribou, moose and elk are all types of deer. The moose and the elk are related. The moose is the largest kind of deer and has a 'bell' under its throat. Reindeer and caribou are the same species, but the reindeer is smaller and has been tamed (it needs to pull Santa's sleigh, after all!). Many Arctic people keep herds of reindeer.

COMMON LOON

With its bright red eyes and beautiful patterning, the loon is part aeroplane (needing a long 'runway' to take off) and part submarine (an expert diver). The loon gets its name from the clumsy way it walks.

SNOWY OWL

To cope with the cold, the snowy owl's feet are covered in feathers, a bit like fluffy slippers! It is one of the few owls to hunt during the day.

MOUNTAIN GOAT
Hooves with rubbery pads make this goat one of the world's greatest climbers. It can survive in temperatures as low as -58°F/-50°C!

WHITE WASH

Many northern animals have developed white coats that act as camouflage, hiding them in the ice and snow.

PUFFIN

This 'sea parrot' might look like a penguin but it's not related. An expert diver, it 'flies' underwater by flapping its wings!

ARCTIC WOLF

ARCTIC FOX

POLAR BEAR

HARP SEAL

ARCTIC HARE

WALRUS

The walrus is born brown and lightens to a cinnamon color as it ages. When it swims in cold water, its blood vessels tighten and the walrus appears almost white!

TROPICAL LIFE

From Mexico, head south into the islands of the Caribbean and you'll discover that color, sunshine, food, music and nature are what life is all about. Pack your swimsuit and towel and get set to explore this tropical wonderland.

GUITAR
MARACAS
STEEL DRUM
GÜIRO

MUSIC

The guitar, the maracas, the raspy scratch of the güiro and the bell-like tones of the steel drum are the sounds of the Caribbean.

CARNIVALE

The Caribbean celebrates many carnivals throughout the year – with a rainbow of color, floats, feathers, dancing and calypso music.

CULTURE

HOLIDAYS

The Day of the Dead and Cinco de Mayo festival are celebrated in Mexico but there's also the Festival of Lights in St Lucia, the Junkanoo parade in the Bahamas and Dia de los Reyes, a Christmas celebration in Puerto Rico.

TRADITIONAL CARIBBEAN DRESS

MEXICAN DAISY

CACTUS

PIÑATA

WHACK A PIÑATA DURING CINCO DE MAYO, AND TREATS WILL TUMBLE OUT

TRADITIONAL MEXICAN DRESS

PALM

THERE ARE OVER 7000 ISLANDS IN THE CARIBBEAN

NATURE

The tropics are a wonderland of beautiful plants. There are endless types of prickly cactus and succulents like the agave. There's the daisy (the national flower of Mexico) and swamps full of mangroves. There are beachside palm trees and fragrant blooms that you can wear in your hair.

AGAVE

WEST INDIAN JASMINE

HIBISCUS

FRANGIPANI

BATS

SHELLS

PINEAPPLE

BANANAS

EXOTIC EATS

Crack open a coconut and drink its juice. Peel a banana, a fragrant mango or pineapple. Smear avocado on your toast. Would you try a strong Jamaican coffee or one of the world's hottest chillies from Trinidad? Or would you prefer a coconut, guava or soursop Caribbean ice-cream?

COFFEE

COCONUT

AVOCADO

MANGO

CHILLI

SOURSOP ICE-CREAM

SOURSOP TASTES LIKE BANANA, LEMON AND PINEAPPLE ALL AT ONCE!

ISLAND LIFE

Caribbean islands include Jamaica, the Bahamas and Cuba, which is the largest. Saba is the smallest at just 5 square miles (13 square kilometers)! With white sandy beaches, crystal waters and abundant flora and fauna, island life is pure paradise.

WEST INDIAN FLAMINGO

ORIOLE

ON THE ISLAND OF BIG MAJOR CAY, YOU'LL FIND FERAL SWIMMING PIGS!

MANGROVE

THE SPANISH GALLEON 'SAN JOSE' WAS SUNK 300 YEARS AGO, ALONG WITH BILLIONS IN TREASURE

SUNLIT SEA

The clear blue waters of tropical America are bustling with coral reefs and colorful tropical fish. You'll also find some of the ocean's giants – the ocean sunfish (also called 'mola mola') and the whale shark.

SADLY, 95% OF THE CORAL REEFS IN THE CARIBBEAN HAVE SOME KIND OF DAMAGE, WITH NEARLY HALF COMPLETELY BLEACHED

DOLPHIN

GREEN SEA TURTLE

PUFFERFISH

OCEAN SUNFISH

WHALE SHARK

SEAHORSE

ANGELFISH

GREEN MORAY EEL

COUNTRIES: 12
AREA: 6.9 million mi²/17.8 million km²
LARGEST COUNTRY: Brazil (3.3 million mi²/8.5 million km²)
SMALLEST COUNTRY: Suriname (63,251mi²/163,820km²)
NAME: Named after Italian explorer Amerigo Vespucci (1454–1512)
MAJOR LANGUAGES: Spanish, Portuguese, English, French, Dutch
POPULATION: 432 million (2019)
LARGEST CITY: São Paulo, Brazil (12.2 million)
HIGHEST POINT: Aconcagua (22,841ft/6962m)
LOWEST POINT: Laguna del Carbón (344ft/105m below sea level)
LONGEST RIVER: Amazon River (3977mi/6400km)
BIGGEST LAKE: Lake Titicaca (3232mi²/8372km²)

WELCOME TO THE JUNGLE

Covering 2.3 million square miles (6 million square kilometers), the Amazon Rainforest is the largest on Earth, making up over half of all rainforests. Most of the Amazon is found in Brazil, followed by Peru, Colombia, Venezuela, Ecuador, Bolivia, Guyana, Suriname and French Guiana.

GLASSWING BUTTERFLY
The see-through wings of this jungle butterfly make it very hard for predators to see. It may look delicate, but this butterfly can carry 40 times its own weight!

A BUG'S LIFE

JUMPING STICK
This curious little creature looks like a cartoon character, with big eyes and a goofy mouth. A type of stick insect, it lives on leaves low to the ground.

ASSASSIN BUG
A bit like a mosquito, this bug uses its long, tubelike beak to pierce its prey ... and suck out all its juices! They're also known as 'kissing bugs'.

THE AMAZON RIVER IS AS LONG AS THE DISTANCE BETWEEN NEW YORK CITY AND LAS VEGAS

PIRANHA
This deadly fish has one of the strongest bites among all bony fish. Along with serrated teeth, it's not the type of fish you'd like to meet while swimming!

PASSIFLORA
The passion flower is a striking, colorful bloom that grows on a vine. It can be used in herbal medicine and is known to be very calming.

AMAZON RIVER
Running over 3977 miles (6400 kilometers), the Amazon is the longest river in South America, and the largest drainage system in the world. There are no bridges at all along this lengthy river! Crossings are usually done by ferry.

WATER LIFE

GIANT WATERLILY
The enormous leaves of this waterlily grow up to 8.5 feet (2.6 meters) wide. They are so strong, they can support the weight of a child. Thorns on the underside of the leaves stop fish from nibbling them. The lily's white flower smells like pineapple. It only blooms for three days.

GREEN ANACONDA
At up to 550 pounds (250 kilograms) and 29 feet (8.8 meters) long, the green anaconda is the largest snake in the world. It spends much of its life in water. Baby anacondas hatch inside their mother's body. She then gives birth to as many as 80 tiny snakes.

MACHU PICCHU
This World Heritage site is 600 years old. Built without the use of wheels or iron tools, stones were somehow dragged up the mountain and cut to fit tightly together. Believed to be the lost city of the Inca people, an American explorer came across the site in 1911.

MILLIONS OF YEARS AGO, SOUTH AMERICA WAS BROKEN OFF FROM THE REST OF THE WORLD. THIS MEANS THERE ARE MANY ANIMAL SPECIES FOUND NOWHERE ELSE ON EARTH

POISON ARROW TREE FROG
This frog belongs to one of the most poisonous animal families on Earth. If an animal is brightly colored, it can often be a danger warning!

HELICONIA
Sometimes called 'lobster claws', the heliconia can grow an impressive 16.4 feet (5 meters) high. This tropical plant is related to the banana!

JUNGLE LIFE

GREEN IGUANA

The green iguana is very good at climbing trees, and can fall 39 feet (12 meters) to the ground without injury. It can grow as long as 6.5 feet (2 meters) and its tail makes up half its length. Despite its name, it comes in other colors, too.

SLOTH
The sloth spends most of its time in trees, and stays still so long, it can grow algae on its fur! It may be the slowest mammal on Earth, but it's a really speedy swimmer. It does breaststroke, just like humans.

IN THE LAST 30 YEARS, 290,000MI^2 (750,000KM^2) OF RAINFOREST HAVE BEEN DESTROYED BY LOGGING. NEW LAWS HAVE BEEN PUT IN PLACE TO STOP PEOPLE CUTTING DOWN TREES

CAPYBARA
The capybara is the largest rodent on Earth. It has webbed feet for swimming and teeth that endlessly grow. Every morning the capybara eats its own poop! It does this because the microbes help digest all the tough plants it eats.

OCELOT
This small wild cat is about twice the size of a pet cat. It can live in many environments – from grasslands to rainforests. Unlike most cats, it's often found swimming.

A FOREST OF FEATHERS

From the warm tropical north to the nippy, barren tip of Tierra del Fuego in the south, South America has some of the most exotic, colorful and unusual birds in the world.

SCARLET MACAW

This enormous parrot can reach nearly 3.2 feet (1 meter) in length. With its noisy squawks and flashy feathers, it can live as long as 50 years in the wild.

WAVED ALBATROSS

The only albatross to live in the tropics, this bird has an odd way of feeding its young. It converts food to an oily liquid in its stomach, then brings it up and feeds it to its chicks!

HARPY EAGLE

This powerful force of nature has claws as long as a grizzly bear and is able to take down large animals like capybaras and iguanas. It can lift the feathers around its face to help it hear better.

WITH OVER
3400
BIRD SPECIES, SOUTH AMERICA IS KNOWN AS THE BIRD CONTINENT

TOCO TOUCAN

The toco's beak is a third of its entire length. The bird can actually direct blood flow to its beak, and, on a chilly night, will tuck it into its feathers like a built-in heat pack!

ANDEAN CONDOR

One of the world's largest birds, the Andean condor's wingspan can reach 10.5 feet (3.2 meters). It likes to live in windy places, where air currents can help it fly high. Its favorite food? Rotting animals.

CAPUCHINBIRD

The capuchinbird is not only odd-looking – it makes odd sounds, too. A chainsaw and a mooing cow are just two of the sounds it makes!

GREATER RHEA

Related to ostriches and emus, the rhea is a flightless bird, around 5 feet (1.5 meters) tall. A fast runner, it often forms large herds with deer or guanaco (like a llama).

KING PENGUIN

The second largest penguin on Earth, the king lives in the far south of Chile and Argentina, the many frosty islands in the Southern Ocean, and all the way to Antarctica. It's the most colorful of all the penguins.

AROUND
72%
OF SOUTH
AMERICAN BIRDS
ARE FOUND
NOWHERE ELSE
ON EARTH

ECUADOR
HAS ALMOST
20%
OF THE ENTIRE
WORLD'S BIRD
SPECIES

FRIGATEBIRD

The pickpocket of the seabird world, frigatebirds
will chase other birds in flight, forcing them to
bring up their recent meal. They'll then scoop
it up and eat it before it hits the ground!
To attract a mate, the male birds
inflate their red beak pouch.

IT'S ALL IN THE DETAILS...

COUNTRIES: 44
AREA: 3.9 million mi²/10.2 million km²
LARGEST COUNTRY: Russia (1.5 million mi²/Western – 3.9 million km²)
SMALLEST COUNTRY: Vatican City (0.17mi²/0.44km²)
NAME: Europe was named after Europa, a Phoenician princess
MAJOR LANGUAGES: Russian, German, French, Italian, English, Spanish
POPULATION: 743 million (2019)
LARGEST CITY: Moscow, Russia (12 million)
HIGHEST POINT: Mount Elbrus (18,510ft/5642m)
LOWEST POINT: Caspian Sea (89ft/27m below sea level)
LONGEST RIVER: Volga River (2193mi/3530km)
BIGGEST LAKE: Lake Ladoga (6834mi²/17,700km²)

MAJESTIC MOUNTAINS

Europe has some of the world's most famous mountains, and the variety is astounding. From the soaring snow-capped peaks of the Alps to the mythological Mount Olympus in Greece, these majestic mountains are the stuff of fairy tales.

ALPINE CHOUGH

ALPINE AVIATORS

Like animals on the ground, birds adapt to the cold by migrating to warmer places, growing extra feathers or fluffing them up, making little pockets of warm air against their skin. They might even snuggle together!

RED GROUSE

SNOW FINCH

PLANTS STRUGGLE TO SURVIVE WTHOUT OXYGEN, SO THERE ARE ONLY ABOUT **200** SPECIES OF ALPINE PLANTS

GLACIER BUTTERCUP

GREAT GREY OWL

ALPINE SWIFT

MATTERHORN
Switzerland 14,692ft/4478m
This pyramid-shaped mountain was made when land masses slammed together, pushing the peak upwards. Geologists believe the Matterhorn was once part of Africa!

MONT BLANC
France 15,781ft/4810m
Nicknamed 'The White Lady', Mont Blanc is the highest mountain in the Alps. It straddles France and Italy, and is famous for skiing and snowboarding.

MOUNT ELBRUS
Russia 18,510ft/5642m
The tallest mountain in Europe, Mount Elbrus is a volcano with two peaks. It's popular for mountaineering. In 1997, a Russian team took a Land Rover to the very top!

SIBERIAN IBEX

THE IBEX IS ONE OF THE HIGHEST CLIMBING LAND ANIMALS, ABLE TO CLIMB TO **9843** FEET (3000 METERS)

RANGING RANGES

Europe's major mountain ranges include the Alps, Dolomites, Pyrenees, Pennines, Carpathian, Scandinavian, Ural and Caucasus.

IN THE SPRING, ALPINE MEADOWS ARE COVERED IN FLOWERS LIKE BUTTERCUPS AND EDELWEISS

MOUNT VESUVIUS
Italy 4203ft/1281m
Vesuvius is one of the world's most dangerous volcanoes. In 79AD, it erupted and buried the ancient cities of Pompeii and Herculaneum. The word 'volcano' was actually invented after Pompeii! The word comes from 'Vulcan', the Roman god of fire.

MOUNT OLYMPUS
Greece 9573ft/2918m
In Greek mythology, Olympus was the home of the gods. The country's highest mountain, it became the first national park of Greece in 1938.

MOUNT ETNA
Italy 10,991ft/3350m
The largest active volcano in Europe, Etna holds the world record for the longest continuous eruption. Its lava eruptions were filmed and used in a Star Wars movie!

WINTER CAN LAST FOR EIGHT MONTHS IN ALPINE REGIONS!

RED DEER

PINE MARTEN

ALPINE ANIMALS
Alpine regions begin at around 9842 feet (3000 meters) above sea level. Animals who live in these conditions need to adapt to both the cold and to lower oxygen levels. They do this by hibernating, moving to lower, warmer levels, or layering their bodies with extra fat.

IT'S TOO COLD FOR TREES TO GROW ABOVE THE ALPINE TREE LINE. THE HEIGHT OF THIS LINE DEPENDS ON THE MOUNTAIN AND THE TYPES OF TREES

RED SQUIRREL

BROWN BEAR

LET THEM EAT CAKE!

Europe is a hub for the sweetest, most decadent treats – from modern delights to recipes that date back hundreds of years. French Queen Marie Antoinette supposedly said 'let them eat cake'. Add tarts, pies, cookies and pastries, too, and you have a sweet-lover's delight!

LICORICE
The licorice root has been enjoyed since 7000BC. Today, salty licorice is huge in northern Europe, and the Dutch adore double-salted licorice sweets called dubbel zoute.

GELATO
Gelato uses less milk than ice cream, but is richer and silkier. It was invented by an Italian chef who served it at a Parisian café called Le Procope. Opened in 1686, it's the oldest café in Paris.

MACARONS
Macarons are made of almond meal and eggwhites, sandwiched together. They might be famous in France, but the first macarons were made in Italy around 1300 years ago!

CHURROS
Churros are fried dough sticks, dusted in sugar and sometimes dipped in chocolate. Some say Portuguese sailors brought the idea of fried dough back from China.

WAFFLES
Waffles are a crispy, chewy Belgian street food that was first sold in the Middle Ages. Light and fluffy, waffles are served with cream and fruit or drizzled with chocolate, syrup or butter.

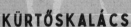

VICTORIA SPONGE
A light, airy cake filled with jam and cream, this sponge was named after Britain's Queen Victoria. When afternoon tea became popular, this cake was one of her favorite treats.

PFEFFERNÜSSE
This spiced cookie, with its paper-thin sugar shell, is popular in Germany at Christmas time. It's served at St Nikolaus on 6 December, when Santa (or St Nicholas) leaves gifts for children.

KÜRTŐSKALÁCS
Known as 'chimney cakes', these soft, hollow Hungarian cakes are rolled in delicious toppings like chocolate, cinnamon and crushed nuts. The first known recipe was found in a cookbook from 1784.

PASTEL DE NATA
These scrumptious Portuguese custard tarts were first made by Catholic monks 300 years ago. Egg whites were once used to starch clothing, so all those leftover egg yolks were used in these tarts!

PÂTISSERIE

TARTUFO
The traditional tartufo is made of choc-coated chocolate and vanilla ice-cream, with an almond and cherry center, but now there are many kinds. It was invented in the 1950s, by Italian pastry chef Don Pippo.

BAKLAVA
With thin layers of pastry drizzled in sugar syrup and nuts, the Greek, Lebanese and Turkish people all claim the baklava as their own. Some historians say this decadent dessert could date back to 800BC!

TURKISH DELIGHT
These jelly-like squares are scented with rose petals or nuts and dusted in powdered sugar. Some people believe Turkish delight was made famous by Bekir Efendi, who made it for Sultan Abdul Hamid around 250 years ago.

APPELTAART
This Dutch apple pie dates back to the Middle Ages. Deep, with a cake-like pastry, it's packed with apple, spices and raisins. It's often served with cream or ice-cream.

HOŘICKÉ TRUBIČKY
From the Czech Republic, these wafer tubes are sprinkled with sugar or nuts. Legend says the recipe was given to a Czech nurse who treated the injured French emperor, Napoleon Bonaparte.

SACHERTORTE
This rich chocolate cake was created by a 16-year-old Austrian chef, Franz Sacher, in 1832. Later, his son perfected the recipe and it's now one of Vienna's most famous desserts.

SCONES
A type of Scottish 'quick bread', scones were once larger and flatter, and were cut into triangles to serve. Today, scones are light and fluffy and served with jam and cream for afternoon tea.

BRESKVICE
These Croatian cake-like cookies are sandwiched with chocolate, painted with food coloring and rolled in sugar to look like peaches. Breskvice means little peach cake.

BERLINER
This delicious creation is a donut with no hole, stuffed with jam and dusted with powdery sugar. Also called a jelly donut, the earliest recipe was found in a German cookbook from 1485.

FABULOUS FAUNA

The animals of Europe are diverse. From a reindeer galloping over the ice sheets of the Arctic Circle to a seahorse drifting in the warm waters of the Mediterranean Sea, here are some of the continent's intriguing animals.

EURASIAN OYSTERCATCHER

The oystercatcher feeds mainly on bivalves like oysters and mussels. It uses its long, pointy bill to prise the shells apart.

GYRFALCON

The gyrfalcon is the largest true falcon in the world. In the Middle Ages, only a king could hunt with this bird.

TUFTED DUCK

This diving duck has a tufty patch of feathers on its head. The male is black and white but the female is entirely brown.

UP IN THE AIR

RED ROBIN

Robins may seem sweet and friendly but they will fight to the death to protect their territory!

WHOOPER SWAN

This large bird has a wingspan of over a metre and can fly an incredible 140 kilometers (87 miles) per hour. Oddly, it likes to eat potatoes!

MOUNTAIN HARE

The brown coat of the mountain hare can change to snowy white in winter.

IN THE FIELDS

FRIESIAN COW

A major milk producer, this large black and white cow can produce 6868 gallons (26,000 liters) of milk in her lifetime.

RED FOX

The clever fox is found all over Europe. It uses its tail for balance, for signalling other foxes, and for covering itself at night – like a fluffy blanket.

FACT OR FICTION?

LOCH NESS MONSTER

This long-necked creature is said to live in the Scottish lake of Loch Ness. Nessie was first photographed in 1932, but early reports of a lake monster date back 1500 years.

LAKE AND SEA

COD

Cod is found in cold waters, and is a popular fish to eat. You may have had it when you last ate fish and chips!

STURGEON

The sturgeon is mostly found in the Caspian and Black seas. It's famous for its fish eggs. Known as Beluga caviar, it's very expensive.

SEAHORSE

Found in warmer waters around the Mediterranean Sea and the Atlantic Ocean, the seahorse is actually a type of fish. Its eyes can move in separate directions!

ATLANTIC HERRING

Another popular food, the herring can be canned, pickled, jellied or smoked.

SIZING UP

WEASEL
The weasel is the world's smallest carnivore. At its smallest, it can weigh just under 1 ounce (25 grams). That's half the weight of a golf ball!

ERMINE
Also called the stoat, the ermine's coat changes from brown to white in winter. In the Middle Ages, ermine fur was only worn by European kings and queens.

GOLDEN JACKAL
The golden is the largest species of jackal. It can reach 55 inches (140 centimeters), including its tail. Females can start having babies when they're only six months old.

COYPU
A rodent that looks like a beaver, the coypu can reach 41 inches (105 centimeters) from nose to tail. The color of its large orange teeth comes from the iron in its tooth enamel (so it can gnaw through all that wood!).

RACCOON
Native to North America, the raccoon was introduced to Europe in the 1950s, and has now overrun Germany (and a small part of Russia). It loves to rifle through garbage, looking for tasty morsels.

EUROPE'S HEAVIEST LAND ANIMAL IS THE EUROPEAN BISON. THE BIGGEST EVER RECORDED WAS A WHOPPING
4189LBS!
(1900KGS)

REINDEER
Both the male and female reindeer grow antlers. Their hooves shrink in winter, and their special noses warm up cold air before it reaches their lungs.

UP TO 9OZ (250G)

UP TO 10OZ (300G)

UP TO 33LBS (15KG)

UP TO 37LBS (17KG)

UP TO 57LBS (26KG)

UP TO 705LBS (320KG)

IT'S ALL IN THE DETAILS...

COUNTRIES: 54
AREA: 11.7 million mi²/30.4 million km²
LARGEST COUNTRY: Algeria (927,000mi²/2.4 million km²)
SMALLEST COUNTRY: Seychelles (174mi²/451km²)
NAME: Africa is thought to have come from the Latin word Afri, meaning people west of the Nile River
MAJOR LANGUAGES: Swahili, Amharic, Yoruba, Arabic, English, Portuguese, French
POPULATION: 1.3 billion (2019)
LARGEST CITY: Lagos, Nigeria (21 million)
HIGHEST POINT: Mount Kilimanjaro (19,340ft/5895m)
LOWEST POINT: Lake Assal (508ft/155m below sea level)
LONGEST RIVER: Nile River (4132mi/6650km)
BIGGEST LAKE: Lake Victoria (26,564mi²/68,800km²)

DESERTS TO JUNGLES

From the smallest scorpion to the tallest giraffe, from vast sandy deserts to lush rainforests, and from tiny villages to bustling cities, Africa is a land of great contrasts. This vast continent has eight major landscape regions, listed here from north to south.

1. SAHARA

Hot, dry, sandy. Endless sand dunes on the horizon – as high as 984 feet (300 meters)! You may see a camel trundling over the sand or a sand viper flicking its tongue. The Sahara region is the largest hot desert on Earth. It makes up one quarter of the entire African continent.

GIRAFFE

A SAHARA SAND DUNE IS CALLED AN ERG

DROMEDARY CAMEL

PYRAMIDS OF GIZA

SPINIFEX GRASS

EGYPTIAN

SAHARA SAND VIPER

2. SAHEL

The Sahel region runs in a narrow band across Africa, south of the Sahara desert. The land is flat, sandy and rocky, with low grasses. You might spot a yellow scorpion or fennec fox here. This fox has enormous ears that help cool it down.

FENNEC FOX

YELLOW SCORPION

AARDVARK

NIGERIAN

LAGOS, IN SOUTHWEST NIGERIA, IS AFRICA'S LARGEST CITY

3. ETHIOPIAN HIGHLANDS

An amazing 80 per cent of Africa's tallest mountains are found in the Ethiopian highlands. The high, craggy land is home to many animals, including the aardvark. The walia ibex and the Ethiopian wolf are seriously endangered.

WALIA IBEX

THE ETHIOPIAN ROSE IS AFRICA'S ONLY NATIVE ROSE

ETHIOPIAN

ETHIOPIAN WOLF

ETHIOPIAN ROSE

ACACIA

4. SAVANNA

Also called grasslands, Africa's savanna region covers almost half the entire continent, and most of central Africa. This is where you'll find lions, zebras, elephants and giraffes. Every year, a million wildebeest migrate over the Serengeti plains.

ELEPHANT

MANGROVE

BAOBAB

ZEBRAS DON'T HAVE BLACK AND WHITE STRIPES - THEY HAVE WHITE FURRY STRIPES OVER BLACK SKIN!

ZEBRA

NILE

REATER

5. SWAHILI COAST

This sandy coastline is bordered by coral reefs and mangrove forests. It's home to the long-nosed elephant shrew and the cutie-pie bush baby, with its huge eyes (ideal for hunting at night).

BUSH BABY

ELEPHANT SHREW

6. RAINFOREST

Around 80 per cent of Africa's rainforest is in central Africa, snuggled into the Congo River Basin. The region is rich in plant and wildlife, including the gorilla and chimpanzee. Driver ants march through the jungle in lines of 20 million or more, eating anything that gets in their way!

CHIMPANZEE

7. GREAT LAKES

Africa's great lakes are some of the deepest in the world. The largest, Lake Victoria, is where the Nile River begins. Hippos, crocodiles and birds of many kinds call the lakes their home.

HIPPOPOTAMUS

DRIVER ANT

GORILLA

8. SOUTHERN AFRICA

This region is home to Africa's animal reserves. It even has its own penguin! The Cape Floral Region is one of the richest areas for plantlife in the world. It holds nearly 20 per cent of the entire continent's flora, including the beautiful king protea.

THE ZULU LANGUAGE HAS A CLICKING NOISE FOR THE LETTERS C, X AND Q!

KING PROTEA

SPRINGBOK

ZULU

MEERKAT

AFRICAN PENGUIN

57

DANGEROUS AND DEADLY

Africa has some of the most dangerous and deadly animals in the world. But they're only really deadly to humans when we enter their territory or try to harm them. It's important to keep a distance and admire these beautiful creatures from afar.

OSTRICH
The largest bird on Earth has powerful legs and long claws. Its kick is strong enough to kill a lion.

UP TO 320LBS (145KG)

AFRICAN ELEPHANT
Elephants are one of the most gentle, intelligent animals on Earth, but if threatened or attacked, they may charge.

UP TO 13,000LBS (5900KG)

CAPE BUFFALO
The buffalo lives in many habitats, from grassland to forest. Its only predators are large crocodiles, lions and – sadly – humans.

UP TO 2205LBS (1000KG)

THE BIG ONES

RHINOCEROS
The rhino's horn is made of keratin (like your fingernails). This huge animal may look fierce but won't charge unless threatened. It likes to mark out its territory by using its own poop!

UP TO 5512LBS (2500KG)

GORILLA
The largest primate, the gorilla mostly eats plants and sometimes insects. Incredibly strong, it has twice the bite strength of a lion. It may look dangerous, but it's really just a gentle giant.

UP TO 430LBS (195KG)

HIPPOPOTAMUS
The hippo is a herbivore but it's extremely territorial and can get very aggressive. Forget the big cats, the hippo may be Africa's most dangerous land animal!

UP TO 9921LBS (4500KG)

AFRICAN CROWNED EAGLE

Weighing a tiny 11 pounds (5 kilograms), this eagle is still pretty ferocious – known as the leopard of the sky. It mainly feeds on monkeys but has been known to take down small antelopes!

FIERCE AND FEATHERED

MOST DEADLY AWARD

Forget the ferocious lion ... Africa's most deadly animal is the tiny mosquito! This insect is responsible for over a million human deaths each year, many of them from a fevery sickness called malaria. Over 90 per cent of the world's malaria cases happen in Africa.

UP TO 159LBS (72KG)

UP TO 550LBS (250KG)

TOP CATS

CHEETAH

The fastest land animal on Earth, the cheetah can bolt up to 75 miles (120 kilometers) per hour. That's as fast as a car on a freeway! It can only keep this speed for less than a minute.

LION

The king of the big cats, the lion is the largest and heaviest. The female is the one who does almost all the hunting. A male lion's roar can be heard 5 miles (8 kilometers) away.

AFRICAN LEOPARD

This big cat is mostly golden, with black spots that help it hide. Depending on where it lives, this leopard can have a base coat so dark, it looks pure black! These ones are called black panthers.

UP TO 165LBS (75KG)

SAHARA SAND VIPER

This horned snake has fangs that unfold into a striking position when it opens its mouth. It's not the most deadly African snake but it still has a nasty bite!

RUTHLESS REPTILES

PUFF ADDER

When ready to strike, this adder puffs itself up to look bigger. It's Africa's deadliest snake, and has killed more people than any other reptile on the continent.

UP TO 1653LBS (750KG)

BLACK MAMBA

One of the world's deadliest snakes, the black mamba is also big, at up to 13 feet (4 meters). Its venom could kill 10 people with one bite.

SCORPION

Most types of scorpion are harmless, but some of Africa's most deadly are the yellow fattail, the spitting thicktail and the deathstalker.

NILE CROCODILE

Due to its aggressive nature, it's best to keep away from the Nile crocodile. It can eat half its body weight at once, and may even eat other crocodiles!

TERRIFIC TREES

The hot and harsh conditions of Africa have formed some pretty astonishing trees. Each one of these amazing trees has adapted to suit the land they call home – from the sub-Saharan region to the island of Madagascar!

BAOBAB
The baobab can be as round as it is tall! Its trunk can hold hundreds of gallons of water. These amazing trees can live for 3000 years!

SAUSAGE
How about a tree that grows sausages 3.3 feet (one meter) long? Elephants, baboons, birds and monkeys love this unusual fruit but it can be poisonous to humans.

THE FRUIT FROM THE SAUSAGE TREE IS USED TO TREAT BURNS AND SKIN CONDITIONS

PHOTOSYNTHESIS USUALLY HAPPENS IN A TREE'S LEAVES BUT IN THE FEVER TREE IT HAPPENS IN THE BARK!

FEVER
For many years, people thought this tree caused malaria fever. But it was the mosquitos living in the water nearby. Amazingly, treatment (called quinine) for malaria was found in the bark of this very same tree!

THE LEADWOOD IS ONE OF THE TALLEST TREES IN AFRICA. IT GROWS UP TO 66 FEET (20 METERS)

THE TRAVELLER'S PALM IS NOT A PALM! IT BELONGS TO THE BIRD-OF-PARADISE FAMILY

LEADWOOD
The leadwood tree has wood so dense, it sinks in water! Africa is dotted with leadwood 'skeletons' – trees that have died long ago, but their rock-like wood remains.

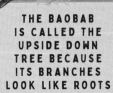

THE BAOBAB
IS CALLED THE
UPSIDE DOWN
TREE BECAUSE
ITS BRANCHES
LOOK LIKE ROOTS

PEOPLE ONCE
USED THE POINTY
LEAVES OF THE
QUIVER TREE AS
ARROW TIPS

THERE
ARE OVER
1000
SPECIES OF
ACACIA TREE

ACACIA
Giraffes love to gobble the
leaves of acacia trees. Their
tough tongues are unharmed
by the tree's large thorns.

QUIVER
The quiver tree is actually a
type of aloe plant! Its trunk and
branches are soft and pulpy but
its leaves are sharp and pointy.

TRAVELLER'S PALM
Found on the island of
Madagascar, this enormous
palm can store rainwater in
the sheaths around each
stem. Not so perfect for the
thirsty traveller ... the water
can become black and stinky!

WHISTLING THORN
Ants drill little holes in the bulbs
on this thorny tree's branches.
When the wind blows, they make
a whistling sound that scares
away animals. The tree thanks
the ants by offering up sweet
nectar, hidden inside each bulb.

TO CONSERVE
WATER DURING THE
DRY SEASON, THE
WHISTLING THORN
WILL DROP ITS
LEAVES

IT'S ALL IN THE DETAILS...

COUNTRIES: 48
AREA: 17.2 million mi²/44.6 million km²
LARGEST COUNTRY: Russia (Eastern – 5 million mi²/13.1 million km²)
SMALLEST COUNTRY: The Maldives (115mi²/298km²)
NAME: Asia comes from the Ancient Greek word Aoia, referring to the Persian Empire
MAJOR LANGUAGES: Chinese, Hindi, English, Russian, Indonesian, Bengali, Japanese
POPULATION: 4.6 billion (2019)
LARGEST CITY: Tokyo, Japan (37.4 million)
HIGHEST POINT: Mount Everest (29,029ft/8848m)
LOWEST POINT: Dead Sea (1388ft/423m below sea level)
LONGEST RIVER: Yangtze River (3915mi/6300km)
BIGGEST LAKE: Caspian Sea (143,244mi²/371,000km²)

ASIAN STREET EATS

From Turkey through India and all the way to the Philippines, Asian dishes and food styles are countless. One thing they all have in common? Completely delicious! Here are just some of the mouthwatering foods you may already love, or look forward to trying.

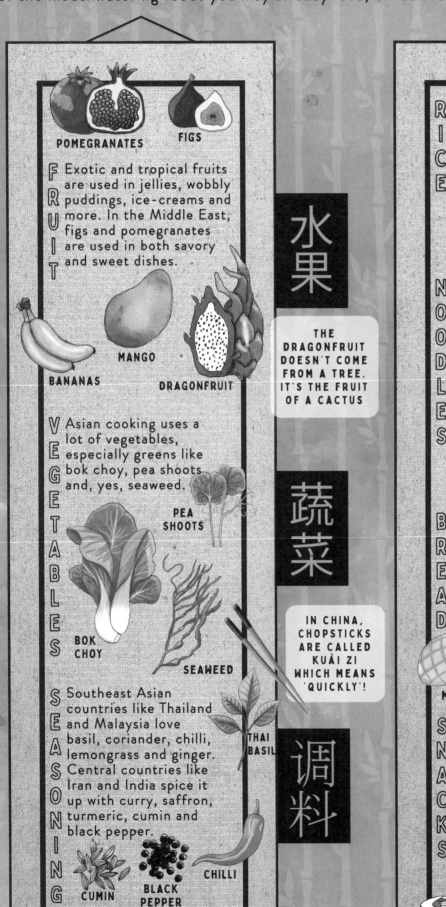

POMEGRANATES

FIGS

FRUIT Exotic and tropical fruits are used in jellies, wobbly puddings, ice-creams and more. In the Middle East, figs and pomegranates are used in both savory and sweet dishes.

MANGO

BANANAS

DRAGONFRUIT

水果

THE DRAGONFRUIT DOESN'T COME FROM A TREE. IT'S THE FRUIT OF A CACTUS

VEGETABLES Asian cooking uses a lot of vegetables, especially greens like bok choy, pea shoots and, yes, seaweed.

PEA SHOOTS

蔬菜

BOK CHOY

SEAWEED

IN CHINA, CHOPSTICKS ARE CALLED KUÀI ZI WHICH MEANS 'QUICKLY'!

THAI BASIL

SEASONING Southeast Asian countries like Thailand and Malaysia love basil, coriander, chilli, lemongrass and ginger. Central countries like Iran and India spice it up with curry, saffron, turmeric, cumin and black pepper.

调料

CHILLI

CUMIN

BLACK PEPPER

RICE A whopping nine out of 10 people who eat rice live in Asia! It's the most eaten food in the world. There are many types of rice, including jasmine, basmati and matta.

RICE

NOODLES

NOODLES Noodle types include rice, egg, ramen, lo mein, udon, banh pho, wanton and soba. They can be slurped up in dishes, like pad thai or drenched in a bowl of spicy soup, like laksa.

FLAT RICE

EGG

RICE STICK

SOBA

BREAD Breads include roti, pita, chapati and paratha. Don't miss soft, sweet loaves like Japan's melonpan and savory, fried flatbreads, like naan from India and pita from the Middle East.

NAAN

MELONPAN

KEBAB

SNACKS These snacks are often sold on the street. There's sushi in Japan, samosas in India, spring rolls in China, kebabs in Afghanistan, and rice paper rolls in Vietnam.

SPRING ROLLS

SUSHI

SAMOSA

米饭

面条

面包

小吃

咖喱

汤

饺

豆腐

ASIAN DISHES HAVE A LOVELY BLEND OF THE FIVE FLAVORS – SWEET, SOUR, BITTER, SALTY AND UMAMI

'UMAMI' IS A SAVORY FLAVOR FOUND IN FOODS LIKE TOMATOES, FISH AND MUSHROOMS

CURRIES Curries are warm, spicy and sometimes too hot to handle! They are served with rice or as sauces, draped over chicken sticks. Types include satay, korma, panang, rendang and tikka masala.

CHICKEN TIKKA MASALA

SOUPS Asian soups are packed full of flavor. Try Thai tom yum, Japanese miso, Malaysian laksa, Indian mulligatawny or Middle Eastern lentil. You can cook your own meat and vegetables in a hot pot!

LAKSA

DUMPLINGS

DUMPLINGS Dumplings are delicious little parcels of meat or vegetables. From soft, fluffy pork buns to delicate pockets with pink prawns inside (called har gow), they can be steamed, fried or boiled in soup (like wontons).

HAR GOW

PORK BUNS

TOFU Made of soybeans, tofu is hugely popular. It can be soft and squishy or firm and spongy, and is served in many ways – from stews to soups.

TOFU

PANDAS AREN'T THE ONLY ONES TO EAT BAMBOO! HUMANS ENJOY IT, TOO, THOUGH ONLY THE BABY SHOOTS

甜食

饮料

SWEETS After a sweet treat? Many Asian desserts are coconut- or fruit-based. Favorites include black sesame ice-cream, mango pudding and shaved ice. Middle Eastern countries are famous for their small and fragrant syrup-soaked pastries. There's also marshmallow-like mochi balls from Japan, sweet jalebi from India, and Persian cotton candy that looks a bit like fur!

المعجنات

MOCHI BALLS

PASTRIES

SWEET JALEBI

SHAVED ICE

PERSIAN FAIRY FLOSS

GREEN TEA

DRINKS It's hot in many parts of Asia, so drinks are a great way to cool down. Even hot tea is drunk to cool you down! Favorite drinks include coconut and sugar cane juices, many types of coffee and endless teas, including chai, oolong, black, green and white! In Japan, a bright green powder called matcha is whisked with hot water to make a grassy tea.

VIETNAMESE COFFEE

TURKISH COFFEE

MATCHA TEA

WONDROUS WILDLIFE

There are five regions in Asia – east, west, central, southeast and south. From the scorching Arabian desert to the lush jungles on the island of Borneo, animals in each region could not be more varied!

MARVELLOUS MAMMALS

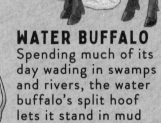

ORANGUTAN
In Malay, orangutan means 'human of the forest'. Large males can measure 6.5 feet (2 meters) from fingertip to fingertip.

GIANT PANDA
Could you survive on only one type of food? The giant panda does! It eats up to 84 pounds (38 kilograms) per day of bamboo, bamboo and more bamboo, please!

ASIAN ELEPHANT
The Asian elephant is smaller than its African cousin, growing up to 9.8 feet (3 meters) tall. With around 100,000 muscles in its trunk, it can gobble 298 pounds (135 kilograms) of roots, grass, bark and fruit each day.

WATER BUFFALO
Spending much of its day wading in swamps and rivers, the water buffalo's split hoof lets it stand in mud without sinking.

DESI COW
With large horns, droopy ears and a fatty lump on its back, the Desi cow is sacred to Hindu people. In India, cow poop is used as fuel for cooking!

CHITAL DEER
This spotted deer sheds its antlers every year. It will sometimes eat its own antlers for extra nutrients!

ARABIAN HORSE
The Arabian is one of the oldest pure-bred horses in the world, and was the first to be domesticated. It was originally bred in the Middle East.

ATLAS MOTH
Found all over Southeast Asia, the world's largest moth has a whopping 9.8 inch (25 centimeter) wing span.

CRAFTY CRAWLIES

HONEY BEE
Bees have to visit around two million flowers to make just one jar of honey! Sadly, bees are on the decline all over the world.

SILKWORM
Silk is an expensive fabric, prized for hundreds of years. A silkworm cocoon is made from one single thread of silk, up to 2953 feet (900 meters) long!

GOLDEN EAGLE
In Mongolia, trained golden eagles are used by people on horseback to hunt for rabbits, foxes and other food.

ASIAN AVIATORS

EURASIAN SPOONBILL
This tall bird has its own built-in spoon! The spoonbill swipes its beak through the water, sensing and snapping up food as it goes.

GREAT EGRET
During mating season, it's the male great egret who builds the nest. At this time, his yellow bill will become mostly black and the skin on his face will turn green.

THE HIMALAYAN MOUNTAIN RANGE DIVIDES ASIA IN TWO, WHICH MAKES ANIMAL MIGRATION DIFFICULT BETWEEN NORTH AND SOUTH ASIA

CHINESE DRAGON
The Chinese dragon has the scales of a fish, the neck of a snake, the horns of a deer and the claws of an eagle. It has no wings, but it can still fly!

FACT OR FICTION?

SCALY AND SCARY

KOMODO DRAGON
The world's largest lizard, the komodo is only found on five small Indonesian islands. It can reach over 9.8 feet (3 meters) in length.

KING COBRA
At over 16 feet (5 meters), this king of the cobras is the world's longest venomous snake, and the only one to build a nest for its eggs. In attack mode, it can rise up a full third of its length!

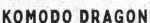

SPOT THE DIFFERENCE

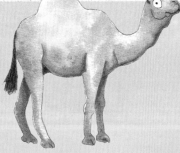

BENGAL TIGER
- Body up to 10 feet (3.1 meters)
- Weighs 485 pounds (220 kilograms)
- Thinner, darker coat
- Southeast Asia
- Endangered

SIBERIAN TIGER
- Body up to 8.2 feet (2.5 meters)
- Weighs 705 pounds (320 kilograms)
- Thicker, lighter coat
- China, North Korea
- Endangered

DROMEDARY CAMEL
- One hump
- Up to 6.5 feet (2 meters) high
- Up to 2205 pounds (1000 kilograms)
- Shorter hair
- Middle East

BACTRIAN CAMEL
- Two humps
- Up to 1.8 meters (5.9 feet) high
- Up to 1323 pounds (600 kilograms)
- Fluffier hair
- Central Asia

A FLORAL FEAST

Flowers are used all over Asia in a range of blossomy delights – from food to beauty products. You might have eaten saffron rice or sipped some jasmine tea. Perhaps you've enjoyed the smoky waft of frangipani incense or worn a hibiscus in your hair! In Japan, ikebana (flower arranging) is a true artform.

SAFFRON CROCUS

By weight, saffron is more expensive than gold! It's used in food for color and flavor. Each golden strand is picked by hand, and over 100,000 strands are needed for just 18 ounces (500 grams). Iran produces the most saffron.

SAFFRON RICE

ROSE

Roses are native to Asia and are one of the world's favorite flowers and most beautiful scents. Rosewater is used in desserts, like baklava and Turkish delight, all the way from the Middle East to South Asia.

ROSE PARFUM

PERFUME

THE ROSE IS THE NATIONAL FLOWER OF IRAQ

CHRYSANTHEMUM

Tea and even wine can be made with chrysanthemum flowers, and the leaves can be eaten in your salad (Dutch chrysanthemums can't be eaten). Japan's annual Festival of Happiness celebrates this beautiful bloom. Its name means 'long life'.

幸

HAPPINESS

JAPAN'S NATIONAL FLOWERS ARE THE CHERRY BLOSSOM AND CHRYSANTHEMUM

TORCH GINGER

This leathery flower is used in foods all over Asia, especially Thai salads. The seed pods are used in fish dishes and the stem is used in curries and soups. It's also used to preserve food, to treat wounds, and for body odor and earache!

LOTUS ROOT CHIPS

LOTUS FLOWER

The lotus is a sacred flower. The flower, seeds, leaves, stems and roots can be eaten, and each has a different flavor! The root can be sliced into chips. The plant is also used in traditional medicine and cosmetics.

THE LOTUS IS THE NATIONAL FLOWER OF INDIA AND VIETNAM

MANY OTHER FLOWERS ARE ALSO USED IN TRADITIONAL MEDICINE AND FOR COSMETICS

JASMINE
Jasmine is loved all over Asia for its fragrant blooms. It's used in medicine, perfume and cosmetics, and to decorate homes and temples. Women will often wear the blossoms in their hair. Jasmine tea is prized all over the world, especially in China and Japan.

TEA

HIBISCUS
The hibiscus is the national flower of Malaysia. In China, it's pickled and eaten, and in India, the petals are crushed into a black paste that's used to shine shoes! In many countries, the flower is used to make tea.

JASMINE IS THE NATIONAL FLOWER OF INDONESIA AND THE PHILIPPINES

INCENSE

THE FRANGIPANI IS THE NATIONAL FLOWER OF LAOS

CHERRY BLOSSOM
People from around the world head to Japan to see the sakura trees bloom in spring. Cherry blossoms can be pickled in salt and vinegar. They're also used to make tea, and in a traditional sweet treat called wagashi.

FRANGIPANI
Used in Indian incense, the frangipani is sweetly fragrant. This bloom comes in different colors and scents ... from rose to plum to banana and spices! The flowers are used in temples, and at weddings and funerals.

WAGASHI

TULIP
Native to Central Asia, the tulip was brought to Holland 600 years ago. In 1637, the tulip was so prized, one bulb could sell for more than a house! In cooking, the tulip's bulb can be used instead of an onion.

BEWARE
NOT ALL FLOWERS ARE EDIBLE. CHECK WITH AN ADULT BEFORE GOBBLING JUST ANY OLD BLOSSOM!

ORANGE BLOSSOM
Fragrant orange blossom is used in perfumes. Orange blossom water is used in desserts and baked goodies all over Asia, especially in the Middle East.

THE TULIP IS THE NATIONAL FLOWER OF IRAN AND AFGHANISTAN

IT'S ALL IN THE DETAILS...

COUNTRIES: 14
AREA: 3.3 million mi²/8.5 million km²
LARGEST COUNTRY: Australia (3 million mi²/7.7 million km²)
SMALLEST COUNTRY: Nauru (8mi²/21km²)
NAME: Oceania comes from the Greek word Okeanos, the sea surrounding the land of ancient times
MAJOR LANGUAGES: English, Malay, Tagalog, Polynesian, Papuan and Indigenous Australian languages
POPULATION: 42 million (2019)
LARGEST CITY: Sydney, Australia (5 million)
HIGHEST POINT: Puncak Jaya (16,024ft/4884m)
LOWEST POINT: Lake Eyre (161ft/49m below sea level)
LONGEST RIVER: Murray River (1558mi/2508km)
BIGGEST LAKE: Lake Eyre (3668mi²/9500km²)

CURIOUS CREATURES OF AUSTRALIA

Australia has more animal species than any other developed country, and most of them are found nowhere else on Earth! Here are just some of these unique and beautiful animals.

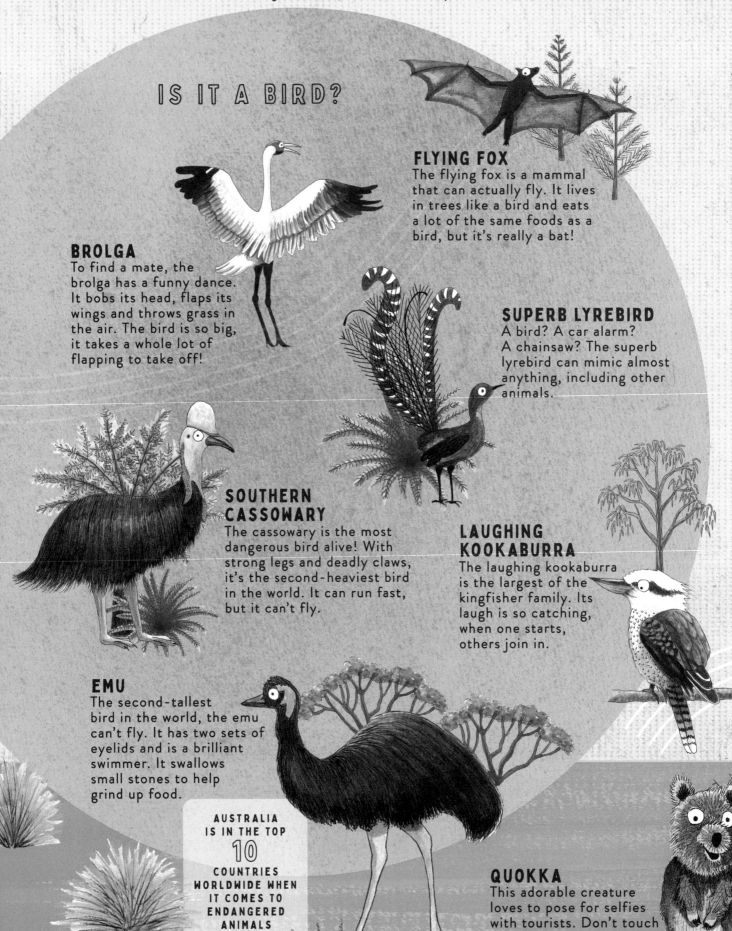

IS IT A BIRD?

FLYING FOX
The flying fox is a mammal that can actually fly. It lives in trees like a bird and eats a lot of the same foods as a bird, but it's really a bat!

BROLGA
To find a mate, the brolga has a funny dance. It bobs its head, flaps its wings and throws grass in the air. The bird is so big, it takes a whole lot of flapping to take off!

SUPERB LYREBIRD
A bird? A car alarm? A chainsaw? The superb lyrebird can mimic almost anything, including other animals.

SOUTHERN CASSOWARY
The cassowary is the most dangerous bird alive! With strong legs and deadly claws, it's the second-heaviest bird in the world. It can run fast, but it can't fly.

LAUGHING KOOKABURRA
The laughing kookaburra is the largest of the kingfisher family. Its laugh is so catching, when one starts, others join in.

EMU
The second-tallest bird in the world, the emu can't fly. It has two sets of eyelids and is a brilliant swimmer. It swallows small stones to help grind up food.

AUSTRALIA IS IN THE TOP **10** COUNTRIES WORLDWIDE WHEN IT COMES TO ENDANGERED ANIMALS

QUOKKA
This adorable creature loves to pose for selfies with tourists. Don't touch or feed quokkas, as they could get very sick!

TREE KANGAROOS
There are two types of tree kangaroo in Australia – Bennett's and Lumholtz's (shown left). They are the only tree-dweller of the kangaroo family, and can leap an amazing 30 feets (9 meters)!

AMAZING MARSUPIALS

KOALA
The koala gobbles up to 2.2 pounds (1 kilogram) of eucalyptus leaves each day, and rarely needs to drink. Leaves don't provide much energy, so koalas sleep as many as 20 hours a day.

THE MARSUPIAL RAISES ITS YOUNG IN A POUCH

COMMON   NORTHERN HAIRY-NOSED

WOMBATS
There are three species of wombat – the common, the southern hairy-nosed and the northern hairy-nosed, which is critically endangered. The wombat is a digging machine, making elaborate burrows with many tunnels and sleeping chambers. This iconic Aussie animal takes around two weeks to digest a meal. Its poop is cube-shaped to stop it from rolling away!

AUSTRALIA HAS THE MOST MARSUPIALS ON EARTH, BUT THEY FIRST CAME FROM SOUTH AMERICA

NUMBAT
Scientists believe the numbat could have been related to the now extinct Tasmanian tiger. It uses its long, sticky tongue to slurp up as many as 20,000 termites a day.

EASTERN GREY

RED

TASMANIAN DEVIL
Found in Tasmania, this aggressive marsupial is actually quite shy. The devil has the strongest bite (for its size) of any land animal, and its jaw can open an amazing 180 degrees.

KANGAROOS
There are four types of large kangaroo in Australia – red, eastern grey, western grey and antilopine. This marsupial is the largest of all macropods (meaning 'big foot'). Its legs act like springs and it often balances on its tail, like a fifth leg!

BILBY
With its soft fur and rabbit-like ears, the bilby is Australia's Easter Bunny! It lives in the desert and digs spiralling burrows to keep predators out.

THE OUTBACK TO THE SEA

Australia is an enormous land of contrasts, and its animals have adapted to suit the various landscapes – from the dry, scorching, red-dirt outback to the clear, tropical waters of the far north. The echidna is the furthest-ranging native animal, living everywhere from deserts to rainforests.

THE MONOTREME HAS FOUR LEGS AND FUR LIKE A MAMMAL BUT LAYS EGGS LIKE A BIRD!

EXTREME MONOTREMES

SHORT-BEAKED ECHIDNA
The echidna's long snout uses electrical signals to pick up ant trails. If threatened, it can dig itself into the ground by using all four feet at once! The echidna's spines can grow up to 2 inches (5 centimeters) long.

FRILLED-NECK LIZARD
Do dragons exist? Well, the frilled-neck lizard belongs to the dragon family! Its frilly neck isn't for decoration. It's to scare away predators or just to cool down.

YOU'LL FIND 21 OF THE WORLD'S DEADLIEST SNAKES IN AUSTRALIA

PLATYPUS
With the beak of a duck, the body of an otter and the tail of a beaver, the platypus is a curious creature. It has no stomach, and stores gravel in its mouth to help mush up food.

DESERT DWELLERS

THORNY DEVIL
This scary-looking lizard is actually harmless. It has a strange way of drinking ... by opening and closing its mouth, drops of dew or rain are worked along its wrinkled skin to its mouth!

BUDGERIGAR
Budgies live in flocks, and like to move around from place to place. Although they can be bred in many colors, in nature, they only come in green and yellow.

HONEY ANT
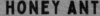
Honey ants feast on desert flowers, storing the nectar in their bellies. Indigenous Australians have always loved this sweet little treat.

SCORPION

Australian scorpions have pretty harmless venom. Northern scorpions are the largest — up to 5 inches (12 centimeters) long.

WITCHETTY GRUB
A rich source of protein, this grub tastes like almonds when raw, and scrambled eggs when cooked!

GOANNA

The goanna likes to feed on dead animals. The perentie is Australia's largest goanna. It can grow up to 8.2 feet (2.5 meters) long.

WATER CREATURES

SALTWATER CROCODILE

The most dangerous animal in Australia, the 'saltie' can weigh as much as 2205 pounds (1000 kilograms), and grows up to 20 feet (6.2 meters) long, which is longer than a giraffe is tall! Its bite pressure is the strongest of any animal, though the muscles that open its mouth are so weak, its snout can be kept closed with a rubber band.

THE AUSTRALIAN SALTWATER CROCODILE IS THE LARGEST REPTILE IN THE WORLD!

BOX JELLYFISH

Said to be the world's most venomous sea creature, box jellyfish tentacles grow up to 10 feet (3 meters) long! It's almost invisible, making it hard for swimmers to see.

DUGONG

The dugong is related to the elephant! Known as the cow of the sea, it feeds on seagrass meadows in shallow waters. Early sailors mistook dugongs for mermaids.

LEAFY AND WEEDY SEADRAGONS

These gentle creatures are a type of fish, related to the seahorse. They are only found in Australia's southern waters. Thanks to their leafy camouflage, predators mistake them for seaweed.

WHALE SHARK

Whale sharks are the world's largest fish. They are sharks, not whales, but they're not at all dangerous. They eat plankton and small fish, and although they have 3000 tiny teeth, they don't use them to eat.

WOBBEGONG

The wobbegong is the only shark that can stay still. Resting on the sea floor, it pumps water through its gills with its mouth. The shark has strange 'whiskers' around its mouth. Wobbegong means 'shaggy beard'.

NEW ZEALAND'S GREAT OUTDOOR

New Zealand is a place of extreme beauty, perfect for outdoor adventures. With two islands to visit, this beautiful country features unique flora and fauna, mountains, beaches, volcanoes, rainforests, glaciers and sounds. New Zealand is also the land of adventure sports!

TAKE IT TO THE LIMIT

If you love extreme sports, New Zealand is your thing! Rafting down a raging river? Zip lining between mountaintops? Bungee jumping over a far distant lake? Let's go!

- SKYDIVING
- HELI-SKIING
- BUNGEE JUMPING
- CANYONING
- MOUNTAIN BIKING
- ZIP LINING
- RAFTING

STEP UP
If you want to go tramping in the mountains, wear your boots. At the beach, wear your jandals.

BAAAAA!
There are just under five million people in New Zealand, but over 30 million sheep!

THE SILVER FERN
Around 80 per cent of New Zealand's plantlife is native. The silver fern is a national symbol. Its silvery underside is used to catch moonlight and guide people home. The Māori people believe this fern came from the sea.

THE LAND OF THE LONG WHITE CLOUD
In the Māori language, New Zealand is known as Aotearoa, meaning land of the long white cloud.

SOUNDS
No, not something you hear! These sounds are deep ocean inlets on the South Island coastline. Take a boat cruise along Milford or Doubtful Sound and marvel at the cliffs soaring overhead.

MĀUI'S DOLPHIN
Māui's dolphin is the world's smallest and rarest dolphin. It could soon be extinct.

LONG-TAILED

KEA
The clever kea is the only true alpine parrot. It loves to steal windshield wipers from your car.

LONG-TAILED AND LESSER SHORT-TAILED BATS
This tiny thumb-sized bat is also called pekapeka, and both species of bat are protected. The greater short-tailed bat is said to be extinct.

NOT SO WILD LIFE
New Zealand has no large predatory animals or venomous animals, other than one spider – the katipō (shown below). This is why there are so many flightless birds, including the famous kiwi. Believe it or not, the country has only one type of native mammal – a bat as big as your thumb!

TUATARA
The tuatara is the only surviving reptile from the dinosaur era! It's nicknamed the living dinosaur. These amazing creatures are born with a third eye on top of their heads.

GIANT WETA
This amazing invertebrate has been around since prehistoric times. It's one of the largest insects on Earth!

KIWI
New Zealand's national animal, this nocturnal bird lays massive eggs – a full quarter of the size of its body (ouch!). To help it forage at night, it has whiskers, just like a cat.

KATIPŌ
This rare creature is the only native venomous spider in New Zealand. Only the females bite.

SAILING THE TROPICAL SEAS

Oceania is rich in marine life. Its waters range from shallow, crystal clear water teeming with tropical fish and coral ... to great dark depths where you'll find some of the largest creatures on Earth.

GREAT BARRIER REEF
Australia's Great Barrier Reef is the world's largest living thing! It can even be seen from space. It's around 1429 miles (2300 kilometers) long, and a whopping 10 per cent of the world's fish can be found here.

CORAL REEFS
Coral is not a plant, it's an animal, and it's related to jellyfish. Coral reefs are vital for the health of our entire planet.

TROPICAL CREATURES
The Pacific Ocean contains everything from the tiniest, microscopic plankton to the largest animal on the planet, the blue whale. The lionfish has spikes full of painful venom. The nautilus is considered a living fossil! The largest manta ray can reach 23 feet (7 meters) wide!

TROPICAL FISH
There are thousands of types of fish that live in coral reefs all over the Pacific Ocean. Many are brightly colored so they can hide in the coral.

GREEN SEA TURTLE

STINGRAY

DOLPHIN

LIONFISH

NAUTILUS

MANTA RAY

ON A PLATE
Oceania has an amazing variety of seafood, from shellfish and molluscs, to many different types of fish. Prawns are particularly delicious!

PINNIPEDS
A small handful of seals and sea lions play in the waters of Australia and New Zealand. They spend most of their lives at sea. Pinniped means 'fin foot'.

AUSTRALIAN SEA LION

BROWN FUR SEAL

AUSTRALIA + NEW ZEALAND

MUSSELS

ABALONE

SCALLOP

OYSTER

PRAWN

AUSTRALIAN SNAPPER

REDFISH

ORANGE PERCH

ORANGE ROUGHY

FLOUNDER

JOHN DORY

CRAYFISH

BLUE SWIMMER CRAB

MUD CRAB

TASMANIAN SALMON

SILVER GEMFISH

OCEAN RAINBOW TROUT

GREAT
FRIGATEBIRD

OSPREY

WHITE-BELLIED
SEA EAGLE

SHY ALBATROSS

SEAGULL

RED-FOOTED BOOBY

SEABIRDS
Seabirds can fly for months on end, without ever touching land.
They even sleep while flying! Oceans are enormous and scientists
believe seabirds use a 'scent map' to find their way around.

GUMMY

GREY NURSE

GREAT WHITE

SHARKFEST
Loads of sharks live in Oceania because most species love warm, shallow waters. Sharks are
ancient creatures. They can smell a drop of blood in a million drops of water!

GIANTS OF THE SEA
Many sea creatures love the warm waters of Oceania. Orcas can measure as long as a school
bus (33 feet/10 meters). The swordfish is one of the fastest fish on Earth, and can move at up to
60 miles (97 kilometers) per hour. The giant squid lives up to 5900 feet (1800 meters) below
sea level. It has eyes the size of a beachball!

SWORDFISH

HUMPBACK
WHALE

ORCA

SOUTHERN
RIGHT WHALE

GIANT
SQUID

MICRONESIA

MELANESIA

POLYNESIA

COCONUT
PALM

MANGROVE

PANDANUS

PALM

TREES OF THE TROPICS
Lots of Oceania's trees are tropical, producing exotic fruits
and flowers. Some plants even live in saltwater. The mangrove
can filter 90 per cent of the salt from seawater.

ANTAR

IT'S ALL IN THE DETAILS...

COUNTRIES: 0
AREA: 5.4 million mi²/14 million km²
COUNTRIES: Antarctica is a continent, not a country – it's managed under the Antarctic Treaty, which now includes 48 countries
NAME: Antarctica comes from the Greek Antarktikos meaning 'opposite to the Arctic'
MAJOR LANGUAGES: English, Russian, German, French, Norwegian, Swedish, Māori
POPULATION: around 4000 people come and go each year
LARGEST COMMUNITY: McMurdo Station (up to 1258 people)
HIGHEST POINT: Vinson Massif (16,050ft/4892m)
LOWEST POINT: Deep Lake, Vestfold Hills (164ft/50m below sea level)
LONGEST RIVER: Onyx River (20mi/32km)
BIGGEST LAKE: Lake Vostok (6058mi²/15,690km², buried under 2.3mi/3.7km of ice)

ICE DESERT

LIFE ON ICE

Antarctica includes an icy mainland (where you'll find the South Pole) and islands, including Heard Island and the South Orkney Islands. The mainland is actually the world's largest desert. The average annual rainfall is less than four inches (10 centimeters) a year, and it always falls as snow!

For such an icy place, there's lots of wildlife, including whales, seals, fish and birds. There's not much plantlife – only mosses, fungi, lichens and liverworts. There are only two flowering plants (see below), and most plants are found on the western Antarctic Peninsula and nearby islands.

There is no native population here, but up to 4000 people a year come by ice-breaker ships and stay in scientific and research bases. Antarctica is fast becoming a tourist destination!

SNOW PETREL

THE MOST GUSTY PLACE ON EARTH. WINDS CAN REACH UP TO 200MI (322KM) PER HOUR

AURORA AUSTRALIS

P&O

THE SKY

THE SUN DOESN'T SET IN SUMMER AND DOESN'T RISE IN WINTER

SHY ALBATROSS

SOUTHERN ROYAL ALBATROSS

ICE-BREAKER

EMPEROR PENGUIN

THERE ARE 18 SPECIES OF PENGUIN IN ANTARCTICA. THE EMPEROR PENGUIN CAN DIVE DOWN MORE THAN 1640FT (500M)

ROSS SEAL

ANTARCTIC PEARLWORT

AROUND 90% OF EARTH'S ICE IS FOUND HERE

ANTARCTIC HAIR GRASS

ELEPHANT SEAL

ADÉLIE PENGUIN

IN 2000, ONE OF THE BIGGEST ICEBERGS (EVER!) BROKE FREE FROM THE ROSS ICE SHELF. IT MEASURED 4247MI² (11,000KM²)

THE LAND

IN WINTER, THE ICE AROUND ANTARCTICA GROWS BIGGER UNTIL THE CONTINENT IS DOUBLE ITS SIZE! THAT'S AN EXTRA 7.7 MILLION SQUARE MILES (20 MILLION SQUARE KILOMETERS) OF ICE

GENTOO PENGUIN

WEDDELL SEAL

MOST OF ANTARCTICA IS COVERED IN ICE 1 MILE (1.6KM) THICK!

THERE ARE SIX TYPES OF SEAL HERE: LEOPARD, ROSS, ELEPHANT, CRABEATER, FUR AND WEDDELL

THE SEA

Lots of Antarctic fish live in the deep sea, hundreds of meters below the surface ... where it's actually a little warmer!

SOUTHERN RIGHT

BECAUSE IT'S SALTY, WATER IN ANTARCTICA FREEZES BELOW ZERO, AT 28.4°F (-2°C)

SPERM

A BLUE WHALE CAN SPEND SIX MONTHS STRAIGHT EATING KRILL. IT MAY THEN GO HUNGRY FOR SEVERAL MONTHS!

FIN

ANTARCTIC DRAGONFISH

MINKE

A WHALE OF A TIME

Many whales simply adore the icy waters of Antarctica. Common sightings include all of these beauties shown, as well as Arnoux's beaked whale, the pygmy and dwarf sperm whales, Gray's beaked whale, the Antarctic minke whale, the pygmy right whale, the southern bottlenose whale and the strap-toothed whale.

ANTARCTIC COD

BLUE

EMERALD ROCKCOD

HUMPBACK

SEI

A FAVORITE WHALE FOOD, ANTARCTIC KRILL IS ONE OF THE MOST ABUNDANT ANIMALS ON THE PLANET

ANTARCTIC SILVERFISH

83

EXPLORE THE FAUNA

Can you find these animals dotted throughout this book? Which continents do they belong to?

ELEPHANT
SEAL

BALD
EAGLE

FRILL-NECKED
LIZARD

BILBY

BACTRIAN
CAMEL

GIANT TURTLE

GIANT
PANDA

BEAVER

KOOKABURRA

MUD CRAB

EMPEROR
PENGUIN

ZEBRA

REINDEER

CHIMPANZEE

HOOPOE

BENGAL
TIGER

KIWI

BISON

ICELANDIC
SHEEP

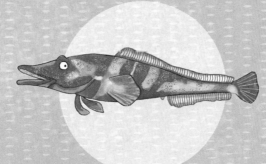

DRAGONFISH

KOALA

AARDVARK

SPANISH
FIGHTING BULL

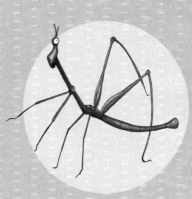

JUMPING
STICK INSECT

EXPLORE THE FLORA

Search for these plants throughout this book. Can you find some on more than one continent?

GOLDEN
WATTLE

PANDANUS

BAOBAB TREE
FLOWER

CHRYSANTHEMUM

CHERRY
BLOSSOM

FEVER TREE

SPINIFEX

CACTUS

HIBISCUS

SILVER FERN

ETHIOPIAN
ROSE

MANGROVE

HELICONIA

TRAVELLER'S
PALM

GUM BLOSSOM

MEXICAN
DAISY

CHRISTMAS
PINE

COCONUT
PALM

AMAZONIAN
GIANT WATERLILY

FRANGIPANI

BAMBOO

ACACIA LEAF

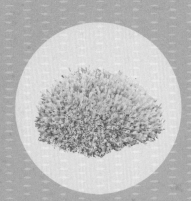

ANTARCTIC
PEARLWORT

GRASS TREE

Some of the illustrations in this book originally appeared in *Australia: Illustrated Map* and *World: Illustrated Map*, published by Explore Australia Publishing Pty Ltd, 2018

Published in 2020 by Hardie Grant Travel, a division of Hardie Grant Publishing

Hardie Grant Travel (Melbourne)
Building 1, 658 Church Street
Richmond, Victoria 3121

Hardie Grant Travel (Sydney)
Level 7, 45 Jones Street
Ultimo, NSW 2007

www.hardiegrant.com/au/travel

A catalogue record for this book is available from the National Library of Australia

I Love the World
ISBN 9781741177398

10 9 8 7 6 5 4 3 2 1

Publisher
Melissa Kayser

Project editor
Megan Cuthbert

Editor
Alice Barker

Proofreader
Nikki Lusk

Trainee editor
Jessica Smith

Editorial assistance
Lyric Dodson

Cartographic research
Emily Maffei

Design
Tania McCartney

Prepress
Megan Ellis and Splitting Image Colour Studio

Printed and bound in China by LEO Paper Products LTD.

The illustrations in this book were created with watercolour, ink and digital elements, as well as mono-printed and photographed textures.

Typeset in Brandon Grotesque Light, Bobby Jones Regular and Bobby Jones Outline.